Diving & Snorkeling

Belize

Franz O. Meyer

LONELY PLANET PUBLICATIONS
Melbourne • Oakland • London • Paris

Diving & Snorkeling Belize
- A Lonely Planet Pisces Book

2nd Edition – September, 1998
1st Edition – 1990, Gulf Publishing Company

Published by
Lonely Planet Publications
192 Burwood Road, Hawthorn, Victoria 3122, Australia

Other offices
150 Linden Street, Oakland, California 94607, USA
10A Spring Place, London NW5 3BH, UK
71 bis rue du Cardinal Lemoine, 75005 Paris, France

Photographs by
T. Brosnahan, F. Burek, J. Burek, J. Conklin, J. Leek,
F.O. Meyer, S. Meyer, B.K. Moore, B. Oppen, H. Parkey,
D. Sailor, K. Schafer, V. Showler, R. Tegler

Front cover photograph
Sandbar by Barry Oppen

Back cover photographs by
F.O. Meyer

ISBN 0 86442 575 9

text and maps © Lonely Planet 1998
photographs © photographers as indicated 1998

Printed by H&Y Printing Ltd., Hong Kong

Although the author
and publisher have tried
to make the information
as accurate as possible,
they accept no respon-
sibility for any loss,
injury or inconvenience
sustained by any person
using this book.

Contents

Diving Safety 38

Ambergris Caye Dive Sites 42

Lighthouse Reef Dive Sites 58

Glover's Reef Dive Sites 76

Turneffe Atoll Dive Sites   92

Hazardous Marine Life   110

Diving Conservation & Awareness   115

Listings   118

Author

Franz O. Meyer

A native of Germany, Franz spent his preteen years in Bavaria before his family moved to upstate New York. He holds a Ph.D. in Geology from the University of Michigan and was introduced to diving while taking a marine ecology course through graduate studies in paleontology. Franz developed a keen interest in Caribbean reef ecology while working at Shell Oil during the 1980s. His first visit to Belize in 1981 led to the development of a field geology course and an extensive underwater investigation of reef evolution. He joined CEDAM – a conservation group dedicated to Conservation, Education, Diving, Archeology & Museums – and conducted reef mapping and photo survey studies, data later used in developing the marine sanctuaries on Lighthouse and Glover's Reef. He became a divemaster in 1989 and in 1990 founded MESU Sea Media, dedicated to reef conservation through underwater education. Franz's other books include *Caribbean Living Hard Corals, A Diver's Guide* and *Anthony and Friends Reef Ecology Coloring Book*. He now lives in Saudi Arabia and visits Belize whenever possible.

From the Author

My sincere thanks go to the following photographers whose excellent pictures grace the previous edition of this guide: Frank and Joyce Burek, Joan Conklin, John Leek, B.K. and Dale Moore, Earl and Laura Meador, Hugh Parkey, Victoria Showler, and Tatnal Starr III. Their contributions are acknowledged, but the friendships we made along the way remain treasured. Special recognition goes to Martha Meyer for her encouragement and steady support throughout the production of the previous edition.

I'm equally appreciative of friends and fellow divers who helped in the production of this edition. For exceptional hospitality in San Pedro, I'm pleased to acknowledge Maria Salazar and her staff at Rocks Inn. My thanks extend to dive guides German Alamilla (Ramon's Village) and Earnesto Bernadez for unselfishly sharing knowledge about Ambergris dive sites. I'm eternally grateful to Joe Miller whose excellent field repairs of flooded photographic equipment saved my dive trips. Once again, I thank my friend Victoria Schowler (Ramon's Village) for dependable advice and help in solving problems. I'm delighted to thank Daniel and Charles, my sons, for their efforts as models and for sharing Belize with me. Finally, I thank Suzanne, my wife, fellow photographer, dive buddy, model, critic, and travel companion, for her unwavering inspiration.

From the Publisher

The first edition of this book was published by Gulf Publishing Company. This edition was produced in Lonely Planet's U.S. office. The editors were Roslyn Bullas and Debra Miller. Hugh D'Andrade handled the layout and created the interior design. Alex Guilbert and Bart Wright drew the maps based on maps provided by MESU Sea Media. Portions of the Practicalities section were adapted from Lonely Planet's *Central America on a Shoestring* and *Guatemala, Belize & Yucatán - La Ruta Maya*. Special thanks to William S. Alevizon for his marine biology expertise, Rick Tegler for providing information and photographs, Larry Clinton for contributing some colorful sidebar text, Marty Casado for his last-minute help and Golda Tillett at the Belize Tourist Board for his prompt answers to our queries.

Lonely Planet Pisces Books

Lonely Planet acquired the Pisces line of diving and snorkeling books in 1997. The series will be developed and substantially revamped over the next few years and new titles will be added. We invite your comments and suggestions.

Warning & Request

Even with dive guides, things change – dive site conditions, regulations, topside information. Nothing stays the same for long. Your feedback on this book will be used to help update future editions and help make the next edition more useful. Excerpts from your correspondence may appear in our newsletter, Planet Talk, or in the Postcards section of our website, so please let us know if you don't want your letter published or your name acknowledged.

Correspondence can be addressed to:
Lonely Planet Publications
Pisces Books
150 Linden Street
Oakland, CA 94607

e-mail: pisces@lonelyplanet.com

Turneffe Atoll Dive Sites 92

Hazardous Marine Life 110

Diving Conservation & Awareness 115

Listings 118

Introduction

F.O. MEYER

Although a tiny country, Belize is nestled along almost 200 miles (322 km) of pristine barrier reef—second in size only to Australia's Great Barrier Reef—and offers some of the best wall and reef dives in the western Caribbean. Between the mainland and the barrier reef sit more than 450 cayes, islets and islands including Ambergris Caye and three out of the Western Hemisphere's four coral atolls—Lighthouse Reef, Glover's Reef and Turneffe Atoll. This guide describes 43 of the most popular, varied and interesting sites these offshore destinations have to offer. An *atoll*, by definition, is a ring-like coral island or reef that nearly or entirely encloses a lagoon. By their very nature, atolls provide sheltered, spectacular coral environments for diving.

Ambergris Caye and the small islands—called cayes—that make up the atolls, feature everything from excellent shallow reef snorkeling to sheer wall diving, cave diving and natural wonders, such as Lighthouse Reef's

famous Blue Hole, a geographical phenomenon whose cobalt blue waters stretch 1,000 ft (305 meters) in diameter and plunge to almost 500 ft (152 meters).

You'll find this guide organized by barrier reef and atoll position relative to prevailing northeasterly winds. The individual dive site descriptions include detailed information about visibility, depth, current conditions and recommended skill level. Each site description includes helpful photography tips and information about what marine life you can expect to see. From the abundant waters of the Hol Chan Marine Preserve off Ambergris Caye to shark sightings around Glover's Reef and interactions with pelagics at the Elbow, the offshore islands offer endless opportunities for underwater exploration.

Sooner or later, however, even the most avid diver must spend some time on land. The "Belize Practicalities" section provides helpful topside information, while the "Overview" and "History" sections will give you a better appreciation of Belize's unique history and rich culture.

Overview

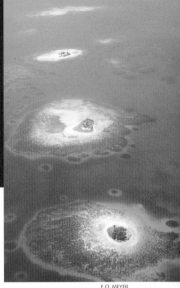

F.O. MEYER

Belize is an English-speaking tropical country with a democratic government and a culturally eclectic population of less than 250,000. Bordered by Mexico and the Yucatán Peninsula in the north, Guatemala to the west, Honduras in the south and the warm Caribbean waters to the east, Belize represents the old adage that great things come in small packages.

Home to 4,000 species of native flowering plants, 250 species of orchids, 700 species of native trees and 550 species of birds, Belize is the last refuge for the jaguar and has, as a country, adopted a conservation ethic. National parks and conservation areas now account for nearly one-third of the country and the spectacular Mayan ruins found throughout are largely intact.

Although most of Belize's 8,970 sq miles (23,000 sq km) is tropical lowland, the Maya Mountains in the western part of the country where lush, wet forests thrive, rise to almost 3,300 ft (1,000 meters).

Belize City on the Caribbean coast is the population center and was the country's capital city until a hurricane in 1961 all but destroyed it, forcing the government to build a new, centrally located capital in Belmopan. Although no longer the capital, Belize City is where you'll find world-class hotels, shopping and transportation to other parts of Belize, including the offshore cayes.

F.O. MEYER

Belize City

CARIBBEAN SEA

Municipal Airport

National Stadium

St Matthew St

St Thomas St

Sixth St

Barracks Rd

Princess Margaret Drive

To Goldson International Airport, Northern Hwy

Belcan Junction

St Joseph St

Belcan Bridge

Central American Blvd

Haulover Rd

Mahogany St

Vernon St

Moss St

Freetown Rd

Douglas Jones St

BelChina Bridge

Haulover Creek

To Western Hwy

Cemetery Rd

Central American Blvd

Iguana St

Raccoon St

Constitution Park

Magazine Rd

Roger's Stadium

W Collette Canal Rd

E Collette Canal Rd

Orange St

Glynn St

King St

Dean St

Allenby St

Barkley St

Victoria St

North Front St

Pickstock St

New Rd

Queen St

Swing Bridge

Eyre St

Gabourel Lane

Gaol Lane

Hutson St

KING'S PARK DISTRICT

North Park St

Memorial Park

FORT GEORGE DISTRICT

Marine Parade

Albert St

Regent St

W Canal St

E Canal St

South St

Southern Foreshore

Belize Harbour

Caesar Ridge Rd

Belize Harbour

Bird Island

Half of the visitors to Belize follow the limestone shelf that stretches under only five meters of crystalline water to the offshore islands, where most of the diving takes place. This guide outlines that same journey.

Ambergris Caye

Located 36 miles (58 km) north of Belize City, Ambergris (Am-ber-GRIS) Caye (KEY), the largest offshore island, is a 25 mile (40 km)-long narrow strip of land and the hub of offshore tourism. San Pedro on the southern end of the caye is the only town on Ambergris and has evolved from a sleepy fishing village into a laid-back international dive destination. Nowhere is the transition more noticeable than along the waterfront. Long docks with fleets of tethered skiffs and dockside sheds emblazoned with red and white dive flags are spread out in front of a thick concentration of hotels, restaurants, gift shops and bars.

There are only three streets in San Pedro: Barrier Reef Drive fronts the island's windward side, Pescadore Drive runs down the middle of town, and Angel Coral Street forms a narrow track along the back part of the island.

The rapid and very concentrated state of expansion in this southern coastal community is due, in part, to the uninhabitable mangrove swamp and shallow lagoons that cover the rest of the caye and render it difficult to develop.

F.O. MEYER

Barrier Reef Drive, with its sand-packed "paved" road, is San Pedro's busy main street.

The Atolls: Lighthouse Reef, Glover's Reef and Turneffe Atoll

The small islands of the three coral atolls dot the warm Caribbean waters to the east of the barrier reef. Like Ambergris, the atolls are mostly covered by swampy mangrove, which provide natural sanctuaries for nesting seabirds and limit the prospects of commercial development. With little available fresh water and limited land space, the atolls remain sparsely inhabited and relatively wild. For the small population of seasonal and permanent island inhabitants, living conditions are simple. As in the past, life is intimately tied to the sea. Fishing for conch, lobster and crab is the main source of income, along with natural sponge farming, although it is not the lucrative business it once was due to disease and intense competition from manufacturers of cheaply produced synthetic sponges. Coconut farming is another venture from the past that still continues on the atolls.

Diving around the atolls is plentiful and varied due to the sheltered waters and rich variety of marine life. Beach diving is possible from a few cayes, but the entrances and exits are difficult because of shallow-water coral growth and rough surf, so most of the dive sites are reached by boat. Offshore boat trips from Ambergris can be easily arranged and the few atoll resorts provide divers with a haven from the tourist scene, along with easy access to some of the most brilliant coral wall dives in the Caribbean.

The Shaping of the Barrier Reef

The narrow strip of barrier reef that forms a long, sinuous line from the Gulf of Honduras and beyond the northern tip of Ambergris Caye has more history than just great diving. In fact, a decade ago oil industry geoscientists realized that the barrier reef line described the trend of a gigantic fault system sitting between two tectonic plates. Propelled by currents deep within the earth, the tectonic plates inched along over millions of years, expanding, colliding and reshaping continents and ocean basins.

Movement along the boundary faults forged the foundations for the barrier reef in Belize. Reverberating motion through the plates also formed the foundations for the offshore atolls. Although no longer active, earth movements along the faults contributed to the development of deep drop-offs all around the atolls, many of which are deeper than 10,000 ft.

History

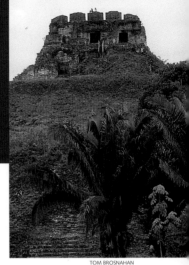

TOM BROSNAHAN

The Mayan Empire

The Mayan Empire, which centered on the Yucatán Peninsula and stretched south into Honduras, El Salvador, Guatemala and Belize, flourished for over 4,000 years. The Maya built huge pyramids, great temples with spacious plazas and designed elaborate pottery and art, the ruins of which are found throughout Belize. The ruins echo the legacy of the Mayan Empire, giving visitors insight into one of the world's greatest ancient civilizations.

F.O. MEYER

Ruins of the Mayan temple at Altun Ha.

Maya Indians were also the first to inhabit Ambergris Caye and the off-shore atolls. Archeologists believe Ambergris' midpoint location along the major seaway trade routes provided a strategic resting point and military position. Pottery fragments, jade, ornamental carvings and obsidian flakings have helped identify many Mayan settlements on Ambergris. Remnants of ancient Mayan "shell-middens" (piles of seashells and rocks) mark trade passages through some of the eastern reefs of the atolls, where archeologists believe the Maya Indians paddled out to in search of new trade routes.

By the late 10th century, population growth, food shortages, trade decline, military campaigns, revolutions and migrations led to the slow but sure collapse of the mighty Mayan Empire. By the early 1500s, the Maya had completely vacated the coastal communities in retreat from the savage onslaught of European colonialism.

The Europeans

The Spanish conquerors of Belize thought little of the tiny country that seemed to have no obvious riches to exploit and no great population to convert for the glory of God and the profit of the conquerors. Far from being popular, the country was dangerous because the long strip of barrier reef tended to tear the keels from ships attempting to approach the shore.

Though Spain "owned" Belize, it did little to rule it, as there was really very little to rule. With other matters to attend to in other parts of its empire, Spain basically ignored Belize. The lack of effective government and the natural land protection offered by the shallow barrier reef attracted English and Scottish pirates in the 1600s. Throughout the 1700s British interest in Belize increased.

Although the British assured Spain that Belize was indeed a Spanish possession, the culture proved otherwise. Belize was already British by tradition and sympathy and in 1798, the country breathed a cumulative sigh of relief when a British force defeated an offshore Spanish armada, bringing Belize under British rule. Sixty years later, Great Britain officially declared Belize the colony of British Honduras.

But, as the Belizean economy worsened after WWII, democratic institutions and political parties formed and agitation for independence from Britain increased, until in 1981, British Honduras officially became the independent nation of Belize.

F.O. MEYER

Today

Today, the unique character of Belize's population reflects the diversity of the country's history. Over half of Belize's population is black Creole, descendants of the African slaves and British pirates who first settled here to exploit the county's forest riches. Racially mixed and proud of it, Creoles speak a dialect of English that is heavy with the musical lilt of the Caribbean.

Pure-blooded Maya make up only about 10% of the population, while one-third of the people are mestizos (mixed Spanish and native Indian), some of whom immigrated from Yucatán during the 19th century. Although English is the official language of Belize, Spanish is the first language in the north and in some towns in the west. You may also hear Chinese, Mennonite German, Lebanese Arabic, Hindi and Garifuna (South American Indian and African) in southern Belize.

The Belizean economy depends on farming and ranching to the west and south of Belize City, while forestry continues to be important in the Maya Mountains. In the north are large sugar cane plantations and processing plants, while the offshore cayes depend on fishing and tourism. Although the two offshore industries occasionally clash, the atmosphere on Ambergris and the atolls is relaxed, laid-back and friendly.

Belize Practicalities

F.O. MEYER

Climate: Topside & Underwater Conditions

Belize is a truly tropical paradise, where the weather is pleasant throughout the year. Its air temperature is mild, generally hovering between 75-89°F (24-30°C). On Ambergris Caye and the coral atolls, trade winds bring almost constant easterly breezes.

Water conditions vary only slightly throughout the year. In winter, water temperature can dip to 79°F (26°C) and in summer it peaks at 84°F (29°C).

Water visibility varies seasonally between the windward and leeward sides of the atolls. Visibility is almost always 100-150 ft (30-45 meters) on the barrier reef and atoll reefs along the windward side. It may be as low as 25-50 ft (8-24 meters) behind the atolls when seas are rough, but most often it is greater than 100 ft (30 meters).

However, sudden tropical storms can cause significant weather changes and can occur at any time. Although hurricanes have been known to destroy the tropical bliss in summer, they are rare. The more frequent weather change affecting diving develops between November and February, when arctic cold fronts from North America push into Belize. These bring "northers," or strong north winds and cold temperatures. Passage of the fronts can disturb weather for a day or a week, creating rough seas and very difficult—or even impossible—diving conditions.

Underwater Wear

Many people dive these waters without any form of wetsuit, but a ⅛-inch (3 mm) shortie in the winter season and a lycra suit (skin) for summer add comfort for single tank dives. If you are planning to make repetitive dives for a week, you might want a ⅛-inch (3 mm) farmer john or full wetsuit.

Currency

Both U.S. dollars and Belize dollars are in circulation in Belize, although change is generally made in Belize dollars. The official exchange rate varies at banks, but the unofficial exchange ratio everywhere else is 1:2 ($1 U.S.=BZ$2). Belize currency is issued in colorful denominations of $1 (green), $5 (red), $10 (black), $20 (brown), and $100 (blue). Coin denominations range from 1, 5, 10, 25, 50 cents, and 1 dollar.

Getting There & Around

Belize City has two airports. The Phillip SW Goldson International Airport (BZE), 10 miles (16 km) northwest of the center, handles all international flights. The Municipal Airport (TZA) is 1.5 miles (2.5 km) north of the city center.

Getting to Ambergris Caye is easy for international travelers arriving by air. You can fly directly from the international airport after clearing customs, as local airlines (Tropic Air and Maya Island Air) schedule flights to San Pedro that coincide with international arrivals. Although not absolutely necessary, it's a good idea to have your travel agent book advanced reservations with one of the local carriers.

If you wish to visit Belize City, or miss a direct flight to San Pedro, Municipal Airport provides a favorable, less expensive alternative even though you'll need a taxi to get there. Municipal is a single runway airport right along the seashore and its small size gives it a personal charm. But, as with all small

A single runway accommodates small planes that shuttle passengers from the mainland to Ambergris Caye.

airports in Belize, flights can land and take off only during the daylight hours. Flights to San Pedro generally depart on the hour and offer a 15-minute survey of the marine environment.

Several boats make daily runs from Belize City to San Pedro. The Marine Terminal building, located just east of the swing bridge, has water taxis that will shuttle you to San Pedro for $25 (BZ$50).

Transportation to the atolls is trickier, arranged primarily through the resorts that send pick-up boats at various times. If you intend to stay on the atolls, arrange your transportation plans at the time you make reservations.

Immigration & Documents

Immigration requires a valid passport for entry into Belize. Belize immigration officials will not recognize proof of citizenship with other forms of identification, such as a birth certificate, driver's license or voter's registration. Visitors arriving by air must have a return or onward ticket.

Due to a newly built airport terminal, the trip through customs is generally smooth. The customs area adjoins the baggage return and although it is small and can get quite crowded, the air conditioning keeps it cool.

Customs will examine your bags. To simplify your entry, have your video recorders, cameras, or laptop computers registered in your passport before you leave home. Just ask a customs official to enter and validate the serial numbers of your equipment before your flight. This will expedite your way through Belize customs.

Upon departure from Belize, you must pay an airport security and departure tax. The current charge is $15 (BZ$30), which the various airline ticketing agents collect upon check-in.

Time

Belize, like all the Central American countries, is one hour behind Eastern Standard Time (EST) and six hours behind Greenwich Mean Time (GMT). Belize does not follow daylight saving's time, so in summer it falls 2 hours behind EST and 7 hours behind GMT.

Electricity

Electric current almost everywhere in Central America is 110 volts AC, 60 cycles, the same as in the U.S., Canada and Mexico. Plugs are the same flat two-prong style. It's rare to see a socket with three holes, so if your appliance has the third prong on it, bring an adapter.

F.O. MEYER

Fresh water on the offshore cayes is limited to "catchment"-collected rainfall.

Water

Fresh water is a major concern for island resorts as most of it is drawn from a shallow aquifer or "catchment" whose recharge depends exclusively on rainfall. Although it rains an average of 80 inches (2 meters) annually, recharge areas and reservoir volumes are too small to support demands. San Pedro on Ambergris Caye with its large tourist volume suffers in particular. It is advisable to drink only bottled water as the catchment water may or may not agree with your digestive system.

Compounding the limited water supply is inadequate consideration given to sewage disposal, causing waste-water contamination of the reservoir in some places. San Pedro is quite concerned about its water supply and sewage problems and recently town citizens agreed to invest in treatment plants. The water facility utilizes reverse osmosis to purify brackish water from a deep aquifer. The cost of water is high. So, until San Pedro and other island resorts in general can tap into dependable and plentiful fresh water supplies, be especially conscientious in conserving water.

Weights & Measures

Despite its claim to use the metric system, Belize's road signs are marked in miles, and gas is sold in U.S. gallons. Both the U.S. system and the metric system are used in general commerce.

Things to Buy

Shopping opportunities are lacking on the coral atolls but ample gift and craft shops abound along Barrier Reef and Pescadore Drive on Ambergris Caye. If you are looking to buy colorful souvenirs such as T-shirts, shorts, swim wear and hats, you will find shopping easy at any of the gift shops.

Various arts and crafts are available in shops or at artisan beach and street displays in town. Belize artisans excel in elegant zericote and cowhorn carvings and in jewelry made from now endangered black coral (illegal to import into the U.S.), pearls and conch. Original oil and acrylic paintings by Belizean artist Walter Castillo and a selection of prints can be found at **Belizean Arts**. **Iguana Jack's** offers shoppers unique ceramic pots decorated with playful iguanas, sculptures, and masks. Divers will want to visit the underwater photo gallery at **Joe Miller's PhotoPro Center**. Joe has an exquisite collection of original underwater photographs for sale and can arrange to ship your framed and mounted underwater photographs home.

Groceries, sundries and other necessities are available at a number of stores around town. Markets carry most of the basics but selections are limited and pricey. Ambergris is an island and everything but locally grown vegetables and fruit must be imported.

Business Hours & Public Holidays

Most banks, many businesses and shops are closed on Wednesday afternoon. Banking hours depend upon the individual bank, but most are open Monday to Friday from 8 am to noon or 1 pm; some are also open from 1 to 3 pm, and many have extra hours on Friday until 4:30 pm. Shops are usually open Monday to Saturday from 8 am to noon, Monday, Tuesday, Thursday and Friday from 1 to 4 pm. Some shops have evening hours from 7 to 9 pm. Many restaurants—especially in cities—are closed on Sunday.

Black Coral: Don't Touch, Don't Buy

Black coral grows sporadically on Belize reefs in thicket-like formations down to 150 ft (40 meters). Although it appears maroon underwater, when polished to a glossy black finish black coral is prized for jewelry. This fragile endangered species may not be legally sold or harvested for export, and unprocessed coral may not be taken out of the country for any purpose.

Unfortunately, black coral is still sold locally. Visitors can help discourage the harvesting of ever-diminishing stocks of wild black coral by taking only photographs and buying other souvenirs, such as carvings made from the local hardwood, zericote.

F.O. MEYER

Creative zericote carvings are a labor of love for talented Belizean artists.

Dining & Food

Cooking in Belize is mostly borrowed—from the UK, the Caribbean, Mexico and the U.S. Being a young, small, somewhat isolated and relatively poor country, Belize never developed an elaborate native cuisine. Each community has its own local favorites, but Garifuna and Mayan dishes and other traditional favorites rarely appear on restaurant menus.

As a Belizean wag once said, "We eat a lot of rice and beans in Belize, and when we get tired of that, we eat beans and rice."

The mixed rice and red beans usually come with other ingredients—chicken, pork, beef, fish, vegetables, even lobster—plus some spices and condiments like coconut milk. "Stew beans with rice" is stewed beans on one side of the plate, boiled rice on the other side and chicken, beef or pork on top. For garnish, sometimes you'll get slices of fried plantain.

More exotic traditional foods include armadillo, venison and gibnut (also called *paca*), a small, brown-spotted rodent similar to a guinea pig. These are served more as curiosities than as staples of the diet.

Accommodations

Ambergris Caye You can find a broad range of accommodations on Ambergris Caye as the island has more hotels than anywhere else in the country. Most are located in San Pedro and are within walking distance of the beach, airport, shops and restaurants. Accommodations generally fall into one of two broad categories: simple or resort hotels. The simple hotels tend to be single buildings whose sparsely furnished rooms feature the cheapest rates, although they often lack air conditioning, dining facilities or a dive shop.

Resort hotels, located both within and outside of town, range from comfortable to luxurious. They provide rooms in large houses or individual cabanas and most offer at least some of the amenities expected in an international hotel, including restaurants, bars, gift or dive shops, airport pick-up, room service and swimming pools. Most come equipped with phones, air conditioning, refrigerators or even a kitchenette. A swim-up bar, Jacuzzi, hot tub, tennis courts, casino and a full array of water sports equipment add to the comforts available at the best resorts.

Virtually every hotel on the caye is located near the sea because inhabitable areas on the island are limited to the narrow coastal strip of sand. This does not necessarily mean your accommodations will be right along the beach though, as many resorts have rooms not facing the seashore. This may

F.O. MEYER

Many hotels in Belize offer dive services and can arrange easy access to diving.

not seem important until you get there during the hot sticky summer and find your cabin lacks air conditioning and is not exposed directly to the cool ocean breeze. First time visitors should ask specific questions about accommodations to avoid unpleasant surprises.

Atolls There are currently five resorts on the atolls: three on Turneffe, one on Lighthouse and one on Glover's. Staying on the atolls is akin to anchoring yourself on a sea of paradise, where you'll stay for a minimum of three or four days, depending on which resort you choose. You can make travel arrangements to the atolls straight from the airport, enjoy a retreat from the usual tourist scene and experience lots of intense diving. The atolls are mostly uninhabited, however, so once you get to a resort, you'll eat, drink and sleep there until you are transported back to Ambergris or the mainland.

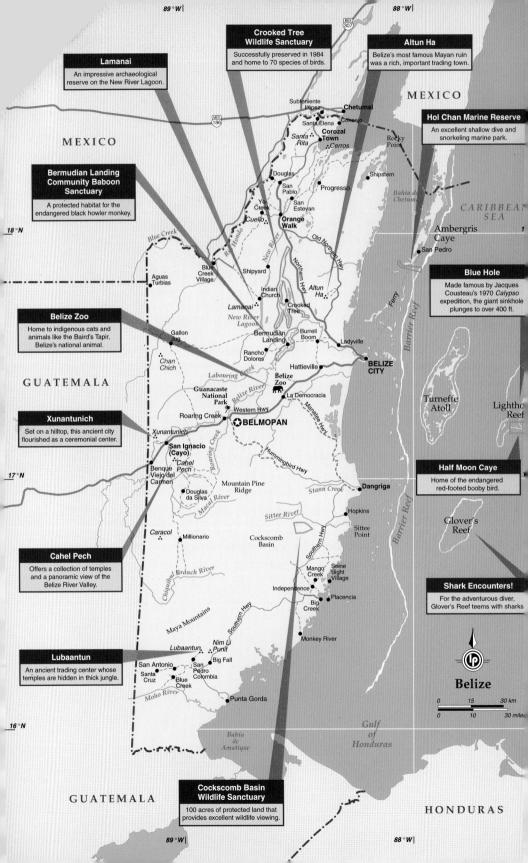

Lamanai
An impressive archaeological reserve on the New River Lagoon.

Crooked Tree Wildlife Sanctuary
Successfully preserved in 1984 and home to 70 species of birds.

Altun Ha
Belize's most famous Mayan ruin was a rich, important trading town.

Hol Chan Marine Reserve
An excellent shallow dive and snorkeling marine park.

Bermudian Landing Community Baboon Sanctuary
A protected habitat for the endangered black howler monkey.

Blue Hole
Made famous by Jacques Cousteau's 1970 *Calypso* expedition, the giant sinkhole plunges to over 400 ft.

Belize Zoo
Home to indigenous cats and animals like the Baird's Tapir, Belize's national animal.

Xunantunich
Set on a hilltop, this ancient city flourished as a ceremonial center.

Half Moon Caye
Home of the endangered red-footed booby bird.

Cahel Pech
Offers a collection of temples and a panoramic view of the Belize River Valley.

Shark Encounters!
For the adventurous diver, Glover's Reef teems with sharks

Lubaantun
An ancient trading center whose temples are hidden in thick jungle.

Cockscomb Basin Wildlife Sanctuary
100 acres of protected land that provides excellent wildlife viewing.

MEXICO

MEXICO

GUATEMALA

CARIBBEAN SEA

Ambergris Caye

Turneffe Atoll

Lighthouse Reef

Glover's Reef

Belize

GUATEMALA

HONDURAS

18°N

17°N

16°N

89°W

88°W

Chetumal

Corozal Town

Orange Walk

BELIZE CITY

BELMOPAN

Dangriga

Punta Gorda

0   15   30 km
0   10   30 miles

Activities & Attractions

KEVIN SCHAFER

Mayan Ruins

Altun Ha Northern Belize's most famous Mayan ruin is at Altun Ha, 34 miles (55 km) north of Belize City. Altun Ha (Mayan for "Rockstone Pond") was a small but rich and important Mayan trading town. Discovered here was the largest carved jade object of the Mayan era—a carved head, representative of the Sun God, Kinich Ahau. The jade head can be seen on the corner of every Belizean banknote. Altun Ha formed as a community by at least 600 BC and possibly centuries earlier. Although most of the temples you will see in Altun Ha date from Late Classic times (AD 250-900), burials indicate that Altun Ha's merchants were trading with Teotihuacán in Pre-Classic times.

Lamanai By far the most impressive site in the northern part of Belize is Lamanai ("submerged crocodile" in Mayan), in its own archaeological reserve on the New River Lagoon. Though much of the site remains unexcavated and unrestored, the trip, by motorboat up the New River, is an adventure in

TOM BROSNAHAN

Part of the magic of Lamanai is captured en route to the ruins.

itself. Occupied as early as 1500 BC, Lamanai flourished in late Pre-Classic times, growing to be a major ceremonial center with immense temples, long before most other Mayan sites.

Cahal Pech The best way to visit the hilltop Maya site of Cahal Pech in western Belize is to take a picnic. Situated along the bank of the Macal River in the Cayo District, Cahal Pech (Mayan for "Place of the Ticks") offers a panoramic view of San Ignacio and the Belize River Valley. It is one of the medium-sized Maya centers and features a small collection of temples, partially restored to resemble their original glory in Classic Mayan times.

Xunantunich Set on a leveled hilltop overlooking the Mopan River in the Cayo district, the ancient city of Xunantunich controlled the riverside track that led from the hinterlands of Tikal down to the Caribbean. A ceremonial center flourished here and archaeologists have uncovered evidence that an earthquake damaged the city about AD 900, after which it may have been largely abandoned.

Ruins of the ancient city of Xunantunich.

Lubaantun Located in southern Belize, Lubaantun ("Fallen Stones" in Mayan) is aptly named. Excavated to some extent, but not restored, the Lubaantun temples are still mostly covered with jungle. Archaeologists have found evidence that Lubaantun flourished until the late AD 700s, after which little was built. In its heyday, the merchants traded with people on the cayes, in Mexico and Guatemala.

Parks & Sanctuaries

Bermudian Landing Community Baboon Sanctuary The endangered black howler monkey exists only in Belize, where it is called a baboon. In 1985, a group of local farmers organized to help protect the black howler's habitat—the forest along the river, where it feeds, sleeps and howls loudly and unmistakably at dawn and dusk. The Baboon Sanctuary is located midway between Belize City and Orange Walk. Contact the Belize Audubon Society (☎ 27-7369) for more information.

The endangered black howler monkey is fondly called a "baboon" in Belize.

Crooked Tree Wildlife Sanctuary In 1984, the Belize Audubon Society succeeded in having 4.6 sq miles around Crooked Tree village declared a wildlife sanctuary. Migrating birds flock to the rivers, swamps and lagoons here during the dry season (November to May), including the jabiru, the Western Hemisphere's largest flying bird whose wingspan can stretch 8.2 feet. Seventy species of birds are regularly seen here, including herons, ducks, kites, egrets, ospreys, kingfishers and hawks. For details about the sanctuary, check with the Audubon Society (☎ 27-7369) or email: base@btl.net.

Belize Zoo The Belize Zoo and Tropical Education Center (☎ 92-3310) is home to a variety of indigenous Belizean cats and other animals kept in natural surroundings. In 1983, Sharon Matola was in charge of 17 Belizean animals during the shooting of a wildlife film called *Path of the Raingods*. By the time the filming was over, her animals were partly tame and might not have survived in the wild, so Matola founded the zoo. On the self-guided tour you'll see Baird's tapir (Belize's national animal) and the gibnut or *paca*, jaguar, ocelot, howler monkey, peccary, vulture, stork and even a crocodile. The zoo is 29 miles (47 kilometers) west of Belize City.

Baird's tapir is Belize's national animal.

Cockscomb Basin Wildlife Sanctuary Sometimes called the Jaguar Reserve, the Cockscomb Basin Wildlife Sanctuary, created in 1984, covers almost 100 acres. The varied topography and lush tropical forest make this an excellent place to observe Belizean wildlife. The sanctuary is roughly halfway between Dangriga and Independence, just west of the village of Maya Center.

Guanacaste National Park Right outside of Belmopan, Belize's capital city, is the Guanacaste National Park. This small nature reserve at the confluence of Roaring Creek and the Belize River holds a giant guanacaste tree, which survived the axes of canoe makers and still rises majestically in its forest habitat. The one tree supports a whole ecosystem of its own, festooned with bromeliads, epiphytes, ferns and dozens of other varieties of plants. Wild orchids flourish in the spongy soil among the ferns and mosses, and several species of "exotic" animals and birds pass through.

Diving
in Belize

L. MEADOR

Diving

Stretching just 12 to 25 miles offshore, Belize's barrier reef extends from the northern tip of Ambergris Caye to the southern end of the country, into Honduras. Because river runoff muddies shallow coastal waters, diving off mainland Belize is limited, so most of the diving is done either from boats or the offshore islands, where the water is crystal clear. The variety of dive sites would take a few lifetimes for any diver to explore— shallow coral gardens, mid-depth spur-and-groove reefs and, because the barrier reef is also the rim of the continental shelf, wall diving is at its best in Belize. Most walls begin in fairly shallow water (20-40 ft) before dropping off.

Although many of the dive sites have similar components, such as lush coral heads separated by sand chutes on the top reef that often form a labyrinth divers can swim through as they approach the vertical wall, the variety in the configuration of the sites and the marine life is abundant. The combination of shallow and deep water creates ideal conditions for repetitive diving and dive boat operators will easily accommodate two-tank trips. Most dive sites are well-known locally and are named to reflect a distinguishing feature; however, you will find that names sometimes vary.

Small cuts in the barrier reef off Ambergris Caye

Spurs and Grooves

As waves erode a reef, portions of its growing front are carried away, forming steep banks that stretch perpendicular to the wall. These coral crests (spurs) are separated by canyons (grooves) with sandy floors.

New growth eventually creates intriguing patterns of tunnels, swim-throughs and grottoes that shelter many animals, sponges and hard and soft corals. Divers dropping into this twisted topography should bring lights and regularly check depth and air pressure since some tunnels can take as long as a minute to negotiate.

make it possible to explore the splendor of the spur-and-groove reef from shore-based diving. The three atolls offer almost 140 miles (225 km) of their own spectacular reef system, rivaling the barrier with exquisite coral rims and patch reefs. Most dives off the atolls are done by boat.

Boat Services

Most of the daily dives off Ambergris are through the services of local guides who pilot island-built skiffs with powerful outboards. There are almost 150 registered guides available to run divers or snorkelers to the barrier reefs just offshore, and hotels will hire freelance guides depending on demand.

Trips to the barrier reef generally depart twice daily from each dive operation and night dives require special but easily made arrangements. In

F.O. MEYER

Dive operations are scattered along the San Pedro waterfront.

most cases, divers will be accompanied by at least one guide or divemaster who knows the reefs well.

Boat trips beyond the barrier reef generally depart from one of the many dive operations along the waterfront, close to the hotels. Charter trips tailored to your own itinerary or needs are never a problem to arrange. If you are staying at one of the atoll resorts, they will arrange boat transportation for you.

Dive boats vary in carrying capacity and schedules. Crewed yachts and some live-aboards will take small or large groups to the popular sites. The live-aboards also offer custom cruises to explore new and infrequently visited reefs or focus on seasonal spectacles like whale and shark expeditions.

Snorkeling

With over 300 miles of barrier reefs, thousands of patch reefs, extensive mangrove areas, and hundreds of cayes, Belize offers many excellent snorkeling opportunities.

By far the best, most varied and seductive snorkeling areas appear off the mainland coast. Behind the protection of the barrier reef lie vast expanses of shallow water replete with colorful tropical fish, exotic coral and unusual invertebrates. Resorts behind the barrier reef offer snorkelers unlimited beach access to sandy areas dotted with small patches of coral, grass flats and reef tropicals. Ambergris Caye, Caye Caulker, Caye Chapel and South Water Caye all support resorts that have private beaches and interesting nearshore snorkeling areas. Another exceptional snorkeling opportunity exists off South Water Caye, where vigorous reef growth occurs only 120 ft (37 meters) from the beach.

R. TEGLER

Readily available boat service to the cayes gives visitors access to the full range and best snorkeling opportunities Belize has to offer. The Hol Chan Marine Reserve off Ambergris Caye is one of the most exciting snorkeling places, dotted with living coral. Swarms of fish

RICK TEGLER

Laughing Bird Caye recently gained status as a National Marine Park
and is a snorkeler's delight.

seek shelter in its shallow waters. Mexico Rocks and Mata Cut are other favorite spots off Ambergris Caye where snorkelers can free dive or swim over mountainous coral formations and a sunken barge, respectively. On Caye Caulker, snorkelers can arrange to swim or photograph manatees in open lagoon areas off Geoff's Caye.

Thousands of patch reefs dot the southern shelf lagoon behind the barrier reef. About 25 miles (40 kilometers) seaward from Placencia, the

Many shallow reefs allow snorkelers close encounters with colorful fish.

Queen Cayes—three tiny remote islands—are well worth the trip. With a cover of swaying palm trees and glistening white beaches, snorkelers can explore exceptionally lush reefs and sandy bottoms teeming with marine life.

Also in the southern cayes, Laughing Bird Caye, recently designated a National Marine Park, lacks the expansive shallow water areas of the Queen Cayes, but is no less spectacular for snorkeling. Great stands of elkhorn coral guard its windward side. Pelicans dive for a catch of the continuous stream of juvenile fish that make this reef their nursery at certain times of the year.

Plenty of shallow water and an abundance of patch reefs make for ample snorkeling on the three offshore atolls. At Turneffe, lagoon mud flats and an extensive mangrove cover limit good snorkeling to a few places on the enclosing reefs. Snorkeling on Lighthouse and Glover's Reefs is no less spectacular than that found behind the barrier reef, including Emerald Forest Reef and Baking Swash on Glover's Reef and, despite its depth, the Blue Hole on Lighthouse. It's difficult for snorkelers to go wrong in Belize. Perhaps the best advice is to set the anchor in a shallow area of turquoise water and start exploring.

Snorkeling Sites

Ambergris Caye
Hol Chan Cut
Mata Cut
Mexico Rocks

Glover's Reef
Emerald Forest Reef
Baking Swash Reef
Long Caye Wall

Lighthouse Reef
Blue Hole
Half Moon Flats
Sand Bore

Southern Shelf Lagoon
Geoff's Caye
Laughing Bird Caye
Queen Cayes

Turneffe Atoll
Blue Creek
Hollywood

Diving Safety

F.O. MEYER

Diving is a safe sport with very few accidents compared to the number of divers and number of dives made each year. However, there are a few basic precautions you should take before leaving home.

Be sure that any personal diving equipment is properly serviced and in good working order. Regulators in particular are prone to malfunction. Carry an extra mask, especially if you have prescription lenses, and check that all of your fin straps, buckles and BC straps are not corroded or worn. If you have done little recent diving, enroll in a refresher course at home to reacquaint yourself with open water techniques, especially before diving in some of the deeper sites.

Whatever equipment you use, you should assess each dive prior to entering the water and, if unsure of the dive details, get firsthand knowledge from a local dive guide or instructor. Dive conditions do vary, even during a dive, and divers should be aware of what to do in any given situation. If you have any doubt about your diving skill level or conditions of the dive, discuss your concerns with the operator you are diving with. When the infrequent injury does occur while diving, it's imperative to summon the appropriate medical personnel as quickly as possible.

Diving and Flying

Most divers get to Belize by plane. While it's fine to dive soon *after* flying, it's important to remember that your last dive should be completed at least 12 hours (some experts advise 24 hours) *before* your flight to minimize the risk of residual nitrogen in the blood that can cause decompression injury.

Medical Facilities

Ambergris The San Carlos Medical Clinic, Pharmacy & Pathology Lab (☎ 26-2918, 3649 or 14-9251 in case of emergency), located on Pescador just south of Caribeña, treats ailments and does blood tests.

The country's only hyperbaric chamber (☎ 26-2425) operated by Sub-Aquatic Safety Services, is across the street from the Island Air terminal at the airport on Ambergris. To fund the chamber many local dive operators charge an optional $1 for each air fill. The small fee also buys divers chamber insurance in case of an emergency.

Belize City The Karl Heusner Memorial Hospital (☎ 23-1548) in Belize City is located on Princess Margaret Dr., in the northern part of town, although many Belizeans travel to Chetumal or Mérida (both in Mexico) for treatment of medical problems.

DAN

Divers Alert Network (DAN) is an international membership association of individuals and organizations sharing a common interest in diving and safety. It operates a 24-hour diving emergency hotline, ☎ 919-684-8111 or 919-684-4DAN (-4326), which accepts collect calls in a dive emergency. DAN does not directly provide medical care; however, it does provide advice on early treatment, evacuation and hyperbaric treatment of diving-related injuries. Divers should contact DAN for assistance as soon as a diving emergency is suspected. DAN membership is reasonably priced and includes DAN TravelAssist, a membership benefit, which covers medical air evacuation from anywhere in the world for any illness or injury. For a small additional fee, divers can get secondary insurance coverage for decompression illness. For membership questions call ☎ 800-446-2671 in the U.S. or 919-684-2948 elsewhere.

Pisces Rating System for Dives & Divers

The dive sites in this book are rated according to the following diver skill level rating system. These are not absolute ratings but apply to divers at a particular time, diving at a particular place. For instance, someone unfamiliar with prevailing conditions might be considered a novice diver at one dive area, and an intermediate diver at another, more familiar location.

Novice: A novice diver generally fits the following profile:
◆ basic scuba certification from an internationally recognized certifying agency
◆ dives infrequently (less than one trip a year)
◆ logged fewer than 25 total dives
◆ dives no deeper than 18 meters (60 ft)
◆ little or no experience diving in similar waters and conditions
* A novice diver should be accompanied by an instructor or divemaster on all dives

Intermediate: An intermediate diver generally fits the following profile:
◆ may have participated in some form of continuing diver education
◆ logged between 25 and 100 dives
◆ dives no deeper than 40 meters (130 ft)
◆ has been diving within the last six months in similar waters and conditions

Advanced: An advanced diver generally fits the following profile:
◆ advanced certification
◆ has been diving for more than 2 years; logged over 100 dives
◆ has been diving within the last six months in similar waters and conditions

Regardless of skill level, you should be in good physical condition and know your limitations. If you are uncertain as to which category you fit, ask the advice of a local dive instructor. He or she is best qualified to assess your abilities based on the prevailing dive conditions at any given site. Ultimately you must decide if you are capable of making a particular dive, depending on your level of training, recent experience, and physical condition, as well as water conditions at the site. Remember that water conditions can change at any time, even during a dive.

Dive Site Icons

The symbols at the beginning of the dive site descriptions provide a summary of some of the following conditions present at the site:

 Good snorkeling or free diving site

 Cave or caverns. Only experienced cave divers should explore inner cave areas.

 Marine reserve. Special regulations apply in this area.

 Vertical wall or dramatic drop-off

 Deep dive. Many dive sites in Belize feature sheer walls that plummet to unlimited depths. Divers should be aware of the dangers of unlimited drop-offs and plan dives accordingly.

Ambergris Caye Dive Sites

Ambergris is the largest and most popular of the offshore cayes, with 25 miles of Belize's spectacular barrier reef sitting less than a mile offshore. The calm waters are full of dense coral and lush reef growth with visibility up to 150 ft. Dive operators making trips to the barrier reef off Ambergris Caye select sites that combine good diving with variety. Spur-and-groove reefs with deep canyons, swim-throughs, and reef cuts are popular and teeming with abundant and colorful life. Thanks to the installation of permanent mooring buoys and natural resource management initiatives such as the Hol Chan Marine Reserve, the reefs remain protected from anchor damage.

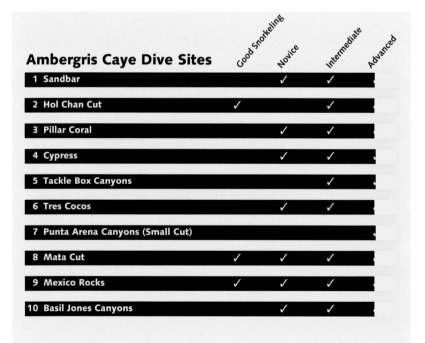

Ambergris Caye Dive Sites	Good Snorkeling	Novice	Intermediate	Advanced
1 Sandbar		✓	✓	
2 Hol Chan Cut	✓		✓	
3 Pillar Coral		✓	✓	
4 Cypress		✓	✓	
5 Tackle Box Canyons			✓	
6 Tres Cocos		✓	✓	
7 Punta Arena Canyons (Small Cut)				
8 Mata Cut	✓	✓	✓	
9 Mexico Rocks	✓	✓	✓	
10 Basil Jones Canyons		✓	✓	

1 Sandbar

Sandbar lies off the southern tip of Ambergris Caye and is one of the shallower barrier reef dives along the island. A mooring buoy line, anchored on top of a living coral ridge, guides divers down to the reef top at 54 ft. The adjacent sand channel floor to the south descends 17 ft below the top of the reef. There, next to the mooring pin, you will find a coral formation in the center of the channel. From the base of the channel, it looks like a tall chimney but it is actually the beginning of another coral ridge that divides the channel into two narrow canyons. Following the narrow canyons seaward will quickly take you to the reef edge. Along the way, relief between the canyon floor and the top of coral ridges doubles from that found at the mooring pin. The floor of the channel here is about 90 ft.

Coral growth is lush and varied on the ridges. Platy growths of boulder, brain

Typical Depth Range:
   50-90 ft (15 to 23 meters)
Typical Current Conditions: None
Typical Visibility: 100 ft (30 meters)
Expertise Required: Novice

and mustard hill coral are everywhere. Staghorn coral, a rare occurrence elsewhere on the barrier, forms in thickets. A colorful variety of other stony coral forms a loose framework that supports a multitude of protective holes for fish and invertebrates. All the tropicals—wrasses, parrotfish, angelfish, grunts, sergeant majors and many others can be found here, but their numbers seem few against the impressive coral ridges. Many more

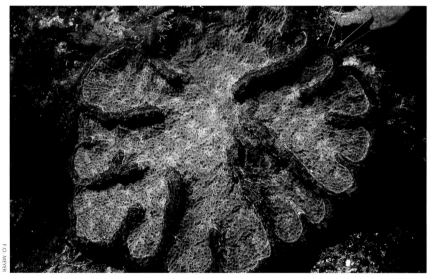

F.O. MEYER

Only four white antennae give away the presence of a coral shrimp hiding beneath the cover of a fat fungus coral.

crinoids, crab, shrimp, brittle starfish, basket starfish and other small invertebrates hide among the coral.

Photographers will find plenty of opportunity to shoot macro or wide angle. A cluster of big barrel sponges in 60-90 ft of water offer good wide-angle opportunities. Keep an eye out for jewfish and other large pelagics that visit these reefs to rest in the many deep caves found toward the base of the channels along the reef front. This deep part of the reef needs much sun, so it is best to visit it during midday when the sun is highest.

2 Hol Chan Cut

Hol Chan Cut, located just 4 miles southeast of San Pedro, is a fantastic shallow dive. No dive experience in Belize is complete without at least one visit.

The cut is part of a 5 sq-mile marine sanctuary that includes the barrier reef, grass flats and mangrove areas. Entry into the park costs BZ$5. The fee helps cover park improvements, maintenance and enforcement costs. When Hol Chan attained park status, mooring buoys were installed and rangers began enforcing regulations to ban fishing and collecting of any type. All the attention is paying great dividends for divers, as marine life has increased dramatically, making Hol Chan a big attraction.

Tidal currents funnel a steady supply of food to filter feeders such as gorgonians, seafans, sponges, schools of grunts and mutton snappers. Joining these plankton feeders are Nassau groupers, black groupers, Atlantic spadefish, cubera snappers and a huge congregation of schoolmasters. All make Hol Chan

Typical Depth Range:
  20-30 ft (6-9 meters)
Typical Current Conditions:
  None to strong
Typical Visibility: 50 ft (15 meters)
Expertise Required: Intermediate

Hol Chan: A Perfect Place to Start

Hol Chan became the first national marine reserve in Central America when it was created in 1987. The name, Mayan for "little channel," describes the site formed by a natural break in the reef.

The Channel itself is about 30 ft (9 meters) deep, with occasionally strong tidal currents. The reef rises to the surface, bristling with corals, sponges, crabs, eels and hundreds of fish species. Night divers glimpse flaming scallops, octopus, and lobsters. Advanced divers drop into the reef's deep crevices, then wind their way to the outside drop-off that is full of corals and gorgonians.

All flora and fauna within the reserve are protected, and feeding fish is discouraged. The Belize Tourism Industry Association suggests: "Do not stand, touch, or kick sand on coral reef systems. Enjoy the view without your hands. A safe distance of two feet will protect you and the reef."

home now that they are protected from fishing.

A multitude of holes riddle the channel walls, accommodating a large population of green and spotted eels. Dozens of eels can usually be seen at the openings of small caves. Eels naturally seek reef protection during the daylight, but feeding by local divemasters has trained them to be more aggressive and has prompted them to leave the shelter of the reef and look for meals during the day.

Eels are not the only animals that have responded to feeding. Large groupers are also eager and snorkelers may be quite surprised to find a 40-pound black grouper in just a few feet of water.

Strong tidal currents flow in and out through the cut and are especially strong at mid-water in the center of the channel. When peak tidal exchange occurs, it is impossible for most divers to swim against the current. Always check the current direction and strength before entering the channel. Abundant soft coral growth along the channel margins makes it easy to read and determine current conditions. Soft corals bent in a seaward direction indicate currents flowing outward (ebb tide) and landward if the coral heads flow inward (flood tide).

Divers can still enjoy Hol Chan Cut even when the tide is running by staying close to the channel sides where irregularities in the walls and bottom dissipate much of the current's strength. Protruding coral ledges and large boulders create current shadows. If you get caught by the current, stay relaxed. Just remember to swim toward the channel walls to get out of the current most quickly. Caution is important and divers who are weak swimmers should probably experience this dive only during periods of slack tide.

Encounters with schools of fish are common along the channel sides at Hol Chan Cut .

3 Pillar Coral

Pillar Coral is a spur-and-groove reef similar to Sandbar. Around the anchor site a coral rubble apron is forested with soft coral. Channel sand, bearing symmetrical ripple marks, attests to the persistent wave surge felt even on relatively calm days. Although coral development on the ridges is similar to that at Sandbar, the shapes of corals are more dramatic at Pillars. About 100 ft southeast of the mooring line in 55 ft of water, there is a cluster of the namesake pillar coral, which spikes upward above the spurs.

Typical Depth Range:
40-70 ft (12-21 meters)
Typical Current Conditions: None
Typical Visibility: 100 ft (30 meters)
Expertise Required: Novice

Recently, Pillar Coral came under the protection of Hol Chan Marine Reserve. Inclusion of this site in the marine park brought about several changes, such as the BZ$5 fee to dive here. A local divemaster must dive with you and, like Hol Chan, the number of fish has increased dramatically. Large schools of yellow chub, bar jacks and yellowtail snapper patrol the water above the reef. On some days, schools of more than a dozen spotted eagle rays pass through.

The pillar coral pinnacles near the mooring pin attract small numbers of schoolmasters and squirrelfish. At the pillars closest to the mooring line, gobies have established a fish cleaning station. Large groupers getting cleaned against a backdrop of pillar coral make especially interesting subjects for wide-angle photography. Divers wishing to include the sun in their photographs of the pillar coral stands should plan to dive here in the morning.

Grouper Interaction A dozen or so large black and Nassau grouper call the Pillars dive site home. They'll greet you shortly after entry and follow you down to the reef. Some will even settle to the

Elegant pillar coral stands extend high above the reef surface.

bottom with you for a face-to-face inter-action. They prefer not to be touched, but do not mind being photographed or looked over, a foot away from your mask. While occasional close encounters with large grouper took place here for years, fish feeding by local guides now make them a regular occurrence. You can expect to see grouper, snapper and jacks swim up to you because they've learned to identify all divers as a source of food. It is a good idea to keep hands close to your body when surrounded by hungry fish since waving fingers may be mistaken as a meal. The marine reserve does not advocate fish feeding by guides or visitors.

4 Cypress

Cypress is a spur-and-groove reef with deep and narrow canyons running per-pendicular to the reef line. Coral spurs crest at 50-70 ft whereas the sand-floored cuts fall off rapidly to depths of 100 ft. The mooring line attaches to coral at 48 ft. You enter the water near the midpoint of the coral spurs. Here, the reef takes on a rugged relief. South of the mooring pin, vertical spurs rise 14 ft above the brilliant white sand floor of the adjacent channel.

Typical Depth Range:
  50-109 ft (15-33 meters)
Typical Current Conditions: None
Typical Visibility: 100 ft (30 meters)
Expertise Required: Novice

F.O. MEYER

Orange crinoids are just some of the many organisms divers can find among the lettuce coral cover at Cypress.

Burgeoning coral growth on the spurs mushrooms next to the mooring pin to form undercuts. Just a little bit farther seaward, the pronounced lateral coral accretion of two ridges has created a low swim-through, which is straight and floored by coarse rippled sand.

Like so many other places along the barrier, there is a dazzling variety of shapes and colors present. Elkhorn, staghorn, lettuce and boulder coral create an abundance of branching, platy and mound shapes right around the mooring line. Huge overlapping sheets of coral shingle the reef top farther seaward. Striking iridescent vase sponges, red boring sponges, orange crinoids, green cornflake algae and a wide variety of tropical fish accent the reef with color.

Photographers will delight in the macro opportunities this site offers. A forest of waving soft coral greets you at the base of the mooring line and is worth exploring for tiny invertebrates hiding among the branches. Here you will also find a variety of juvenile fish among the dense stands of lettuce coral. Dusky damselfish, rock beauties, french angelfish, hogfish, spiny lobster and hermit crabs wait to have their portraits taken.

F. BUREK

Shrimp come out at night and make excellent macro photography subjects as they rest on soft coral backdrops.

5 Tackle Box Canyons

If you want photographs of divers in tunnel mouths or descending through gaps in cavern roofs, Tackle Box Canyons is your dive site. Named after the Tackle Box bar situated directly onshore, this site features several deep, narrow canyons with vertical walls.

Typical Depth Range:
  66-100 ft (20-30 meters)
Typical Current Conditions: None
Typical Visibility: 100 ft (30 meters)
Expertise Required: Intermediate

As with most dive sites near San Pedro, Tackle Box Canyons has a mooring buoy that provides dependable access to the rugged reef terrain on this part of the barrier. By following the narrow channel next to the mooring line seaward, you will come across a short tunnel decorated with sponges and other colorful encrusting organisms. Beyond it is a cavern with a gap in its roof, large enough for a diver to pass through.

Marine life is generally sparse and unpredictable in the caves and tunnels. Lobsters regularly take advantage of the protective recesses and horse-eye jacks may gather in the upper reaches of partially roofed-over caverns. Another resident seen here is the nocturnal glassy sweeper. This small fish with oversize eyes typically congregates in the darkness found just inside small cave mouths.

While marine life is sporadic in the depths and shadows of these deep canyons, it is abundant on top of the coral ridges. Large plates of boulder coral, heads of brain, yellow pencil, mustard hill and isolated stands of elkhorn coral form the ridges. Iridescent vase, basket and rope sponges adorn the coral formations. Bright red boring sponges, orange crinoids, green and red algae add color, while the usual range of tropical fish, eels and other mobile animals enliven the reef with movement.

Years of vertical coral growth means high-profile reefs with deep, narrow channels.

F.O. MEYER

The tops of coral spurs are crowded with algae, corals, sponges and a host of tiny invertebrates that hide beneath the plant and coral canopy.

6 Tres Cocos

Typical Depth Range:
  50-100 ft (15-30 meters)
Typical Current Conditions: None
Typical Visibility: 100 ft (30 meters)
Expertise Required: Novice

If you want to keep your boat ride to a minimum and still dive a spectacular reef, Tres Cocos is for you. It only takes five minutes to get there out of San Pedro. The mooring buoy is a short distance beyond the protection of the reef, which can be helpful on rough days.

Tres Cocos is a spur-and-groove reef with deep and locally narrow canyons running perpendicular to the reef line. It is similar to Cypress in depth and relief. The coral spurs crest at 50-80 ft whereas the sand-floored canyons fall off rapidly to depths of 110 ft. Like a giant plowed furrow, the canyon and coral formations run straight and true. If you follow the mooring line down it will lead you to a spur covered with a forest of soft corals swaying to the rhythm of the ever-present wave surge.

Tres Cocos offers a menagerie of marine life. Even without leaving the vicinity of the anchor line you can see more than 50 different kinds of fish, coral and other invertebrates. Here harlequin bass, trumpetfish, French grunts, dusky damselfish, porkfish, blue chromis, schoolmasters, stoplight parrotfish and squirrelfish commonly dart among the coral cover. Yellowtail snapper, gray angelfish, bar jacks, black durgeon and Atlantic spadefish patrol the waters just above the reefs or in the canyons. Lettuce, boulder, brain, pencil, blushing star, club finger, mustard hill and staghorn coral are only a partial list of the reef builders found here. Colorful sponges, delicate orange crinoids and branching anemones add to the list of marine life.

Photographers must decide between macro or wide-angle here. Both offer great opportunities. South of the mooring pin (right if facing seaward) a vase sponge and large flower coral combination make a great wide angle shot along the spur's rim. Elsewhere along the rim are colorful rope sponges perfect for accenting diver portraits or a colorful backdrop for macro photographers. Encrusting sponges and red algae completely paint the vertical spur walls red and purple. A host of small invertebrates, which shelter among the many holes in this part of the reef, stand out in stark contrast to the colorful background.

F.O. MEYER

A magnificent coral and sponge garden covers the reef ridges at Tres Cocos.

7 Punta Arena Canyons (Small Cut)

Punta Arena Canyons (also called Small Cut by some guides) is located directly offshore from the Belizean Hotel. Getting there involves negotiating a narrow passage through the barrier. During rough weather, it is difficult to make it to the dive site.

This is a deep cavern dive with vertically walled canyons, tunnels, caves and deep intervening sand channels. The tops of coral ridges are mostly in the range of 60-75 ft, but tunnel investigation takes you below 90 ft. Exploration of a narrow tunnel a short two canyons north of the entry point is the main attraction. Its entrance is a gaping triangular opening at the base of a coral ridge. It is large enough to accommodate two divers side by side, but the passageway is not. The tunnel winds through the reef for about 75 ft to an exit point at 100 ft. Sand floors the tunnel bottom along its entire length, so visibility loss from re-sedimentation is generally not a problem. However, parts of the tunnel fall into total darkness because of its length and a right-hand bend some distance before the exit point.

Caution: Red algae seemingly thrives in the low light conditions of the tunnel. It encrusts the tunnel walls extensively. Be careful negotiating the narrow passageway. The algae has a rugged and abrasive skeleton capable of leaving nasty gashes on divers who carelessly scrape the cavern walls.

Not many organisms live inside the passageway. Glassy sweepers, a nocturnal fish, are an exception and a small school generally mills about just inside the tunnel's exit point. On occasion turtles, jewfish and nurse sharks come here to rest in the protective confines of the tunnel.

Typical Depth Range:
60-100 ft (18-30 meters)
Typical Current Conditions:
None to mild southerly
Typical Visibility: 100 ft (30 meters)
Expertise Required:
Advanced with specialized training in deep diving

F.O. MEYER

Bring a flashlight as little light enters the deep, narrow tunnel at Punta Arena.

8 Mata Cut

Another pass through the barrier reef, known as Mata Cut, occurs just a few miles north of Punta Arena Canyons. Remains of an old barge some call *Changa's Wreck* lies just inside the reef in less than 10 ft of water. A variety of soft corals and encrusting sponges decorate the barge's frame and the rusted out hull is a hang-out for a small school of snappers. It's a great place to combine fish and wreck photography. Especially dramatic scenes exist when the midday sun sends shafts of light through holes in the hull.

Resting just behind the reef but within the cut, the wreck lies in water that can get rough. Even on calm days, the incoming ocean swells passing through the cut create mild currents and wave surge. Water conditions get significantly worse when the prevailing northeasterly winds are strong. During such periods, a wave surge scours the sandy bottom and suspends clouds of sediment in the water column.

Typical Depth Range:
    8-16 ft (2-5 meters)
Typical Current Conditions:
    None to mild
Typical Visibility: 50 ft (15 meters)
Expertise Required: Novice

Near the barge are sand, grass and coral flats. You can find stingrays searching for crustaceans and mollusks on the sand flats. Large orange and red starfish prowl the turtle grass areas for clams. Conches of all sizes reside on the grass meadows. Scattered soft and hard coral formations create a third biotic zone. Colorful tropical reef fish can be seen everywhere among the coral. Stoplight parrotfish, trumpetfish, bluestriped grunts, triggerfish, blue tang and rock beauties are an abbreviated list of what is here.

F.O. MEYER

The remains of an old barge rest inside the reef and are home to several species of fish.

9 Mexico Rocks

A 20-minute skiff ride north of San Pedro brings you to the well-known cluster of coral heads called Mexico Rocks. No mooring buoys mark this site, but all the locals know its location adjacent to the former coconut plantation named Mexico Cocal. Shallow and protected by the barrier reef from ocean swells, this site is great for snorkelers and divers. It's shallow enough so snorkelers can see without diving and divers can maximize their bottom time. "Rusty" divers will appreciate its benign conditions to refresh their skills before taking on the deeper sites of the barrier reef. With its shallow conditions and favorable light, photographers can concentrate on composition all day long.

Although the reef is not as magnificent as the barrier, the scattered coral heads and marine life make impressive wide angle and macro subjects. Truck size colonies of boulder coral 10-12 ft high nearly reach the surface and provide refuge to a variety of marine life. Flame scallops, anemones, tube worms, shrimp and eels shelter in the coral nooks and crannies. Sea fans, azure vase sponges, butterflyfish and wrasses add additional life and color. Bluestriped grunts especially like the soft coral stands of open sand areas and seek shelter among the tangled branches when approached. Be sure not to pass up the sand flats for macro possibilities. You need to get right

Typical Depth Range:
8-12 ft (2-4 meters)
Typical Current Conditions: None
Typical Visibility: 50 ft (15 meters)
Expertise Required: Novice

down on the sand to see tiny mysid shrimp, hermit crabs and clams. A little detective work will reward you with burrowed urchins, brittle starfish and other organisms that shelter or feed in the sediment.

Large purple gorgonians festooned on giant boulder coral sway with the waves at Mexico Rocks.

At night the reef octopus searches for a dish of mollusks.

This tiny orange crab is one of many unusual invertebrates found on sea fans.

10 Basil Jones Canyons

Typical Depth Range:
15-70 ft (5-21 meters)
Typical Current Conditions: None
Typical Visibility: 50 ft (15 meters)
Expertise Required: Novice

Basil Jones is a spur-and-groove reef outside the last pass before the barrier meets the north end of Ambergris Caye. Located about 45 minutes north of San Pedro, this part of the barrier reef lies beyond the normal range of dive sites. It takes calm seas and special arrangements to reach Basil Jones Canyons because you can only get there by boat. Should you decide to do this dive, be prepared to start early, pay for the extra fuel and make a full day of it. Bring along lunch and extra tanks. A completely private sandy beach perfect for a picnic awaits you, and the lagoon behind the reef lets you spend your surface interval time snorkeling. The back reef is shallow and packed with attractions not seen elsewhere because the barrier at Basil Jones forms close to the island.

Lens-shaped coral stacks and wide sand flats characterize the reef at Basil Jones, but it is the potential of seeing large pelagics that make it worth the effort to get there. Basil Jones lies beyond the normal reach of fishing boats creating a natural refuge for marine life. Many coral formations around the sand flats feature overhangs with ceilings that are 3-8 ft high. Lobsters are particularly fond of these recesses and they attract hungry Nassau and black groupers. Nurse sharks rest in the canyons, stingrays root through broad sand flats

and turtle, jewfish, eagle and manta rays patrol the water above the reef.

Giant boulder corals mantle the reef surface at Basil Jones.

F.O. MEYER

Lighthouse Reef Dive Sites

Lighthouse is the farthest atoll from shore and offers some of the best underwater visibility in Belize. Exquisite reef formations and walls beginning as shallow as 35 ft are draped with colorful sponges and corals that burst through the crystal clear water. The famous Blue Hole, a seemingly limitless turquoise lagoon in the middle of Lighthouse Reef, is a unique experience you won't want to miss. Some of the most spectacular wall dives exist on Lighthouse, including a series of shallow drop-offs on the ocean side of Half Moon Caye, where excellent opportunities exist for both land and water exploration.

Lighthouse Reef Dive Sites	Good Snorkeling	Novice	Intermediate	Advanced
11 Hat Caye Drop-off		✓	✓	✓
12 Tres Cocos		✓	✓	✓
13 Long Caye Ridge		✓	✓	✓
14 Que Brada		✓	✓	✓
15 Cathedral Reef			✓	✓
16 Silver Caves			✓	✓
17 The Aquarium			✓	✓
18 Nurse Shark Lodge			✓	✓
19 Eagle Ray Wall	✓		✓	✓
20 Southwest Cut			✓	✓
21 West Point I & II		✓	✓	✓
22 Half Moon Wall			✓	✓
23 Blue Hole	✓			✓

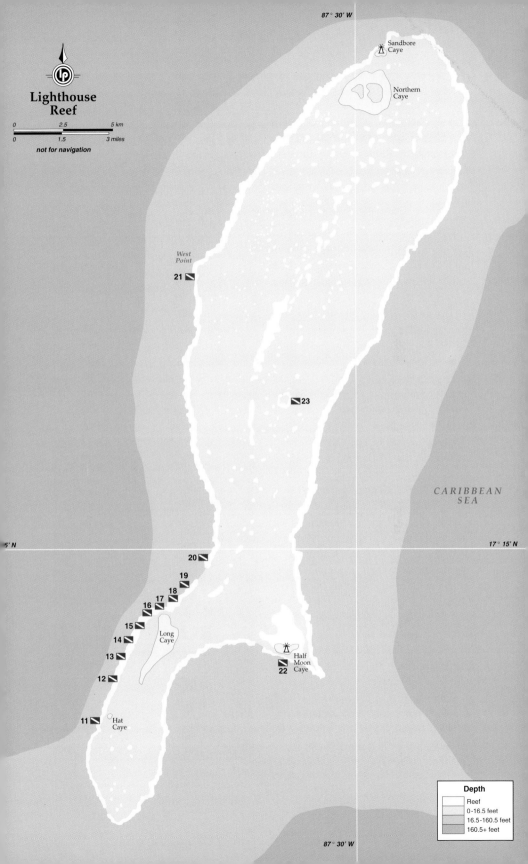

Lighthouse
Reef

0   2.5   5 km
0   1.5   3 miles

not for navigation

87° 30' W

Sandbore
Cave

Northern
Cave

West
Point

21

23

CARIBBEAN
SEA

5' N   17° 15' N

20

19

18

17

16

15

Long Cave

14

13   Half
                                                     Moon
12   Cave

                                                     22

11   Hat
        Cave

87° 30' W

Depth

	Reef
	0-16.5 feet
	16.5-160.5 feet
	160.5+ feet

11 Hat Caye Drop-off

A short distance west from a tiny island called Hat Caye is a reef drop-off that bears its name. Situated along the main wall in the western limb of Lighthouse Reef, it has an interesting shallow reef and is the southernmost site dive boats regularly visit on this atoll.

The shallow reef is wide, with an extensive patch of sloping sand separating two reefs: a very shallow reef near the island and a narrow line of reefs that hug the drop-off at 50 ft.

Dive boats typically anchor above the sloping sand areas close to the wall. Both the drop-off and adjoining reefs offer some exciting diving with dramatic wide-angle photographic possibilities, but the sandy slope behind the reef rimming the wall should not be ignored. It has some unique marine life.

Along the rim of Hat Caye Drop-off are some huge basket sponges, the largest quite capable of completely hiding a diver. In the midst of such grandeur, many divers feel the need to climb inside the cavernous sponge opening. However sponges, which take a long time to grow, invariably get damaged by fins, tanks, or hands during such maneuvers. Damaged sponge tissue is susceptible to disease, which can eventually kill the sponge.

Basket sponges are also home to many other animals and their rough exterior surface should be checked over carefully. Brittle starfish by the hundreds are quite common, but during the day most hide in the deep pits of the sponge. Often, only a few hairy starfish arms can be seen wrapped around the many knobby external sponge growths. Look here for white antennae that belong to the red and white coral shrimp.

Typical Depth Range:
 50 ft (15 meters) to unlimited (wall)
Typical Current Conditions:
 None to minimal
Typical Visibility: 50 ft (15 meters)
Expertise Required: Novice

The drop-off also has several other major marine life attractions, including an abundance of deep-water lace coral, giant yellow tube sponges and lots of fish. You may have to do several dives here to appreciate everything this site has to offer.

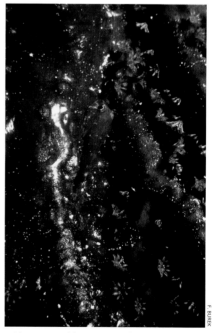

F. BUREK

Almost invisible against a deep-water lace coral, the clingfish eludes its predators.

12 Tres Cocos

Named for a cluster of three tall coconut palm trees due east on Long Caye, this reef lies about 1 mile north of Hat Caye Drop-off. It is the second of a series of superb dive sites found on the main western reef line of Lighthouse. The first of its many attractions is a shallow coral reef and wall with some large overhangs. Although algae cover much of the shallow reef, you'll find a satisfying collection of other marine life. Large spotted moray eels, lion's paw sea cucumbers, several kinds of urchins, coral shrimp, arrow crabs and sea feathers are just some examples of the invertebrates that seek refuge here. Cowfish scull around patches of coral and juvenile jackknife-fish stay close to the protective holes found everywhere on the reef. A host of damselfish, parrotfish and

Typical Depth Range:
30 ft (9 meters) to unlimited (wall)
Typical Current Conditions:
Minimal to moderate
Typical Visibility: 80 ft (24 meters)
Expertise Required: Novice

blue tang are attracted by the algal lawn, and schools of jacks share the water above the reef with very large and hungry black groupers.

Black coral bushes develop on the wall at 30 ft. Turtles are common visitors,

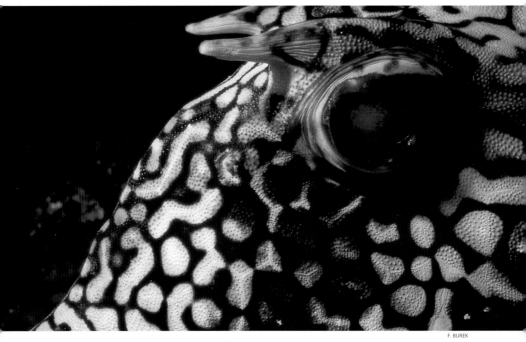

F. BUREK

Honeycomb cowfish are notoriously poor swimmers and those at Tres Cocos let you get close enough to see their horns.

coming here to graze algae on the sand slopes, while Spanish mackerels and Creole wrasses look for food just off the wall.

Following the wall northward, divers will discover large sand flats replace the reef and a wall enhanced with beautiful coral arches 30-40 ft below the surface. Conch, rays and peacock flounders are the main attractions on the sand flats. Graceful tube sponges and delicate soft corals hang elegantly from the arches and wall. At 45-65 ft, divers can find small schools of blackcap basslets close to or under the overhangs.

On exceptional days, this part of Tres Cocos offers some of the most dramatic and colorful underwater photography possibilities found anywhere in Belize.

Divers will discover many unusual invertebrates hidden among the coral growth.

13 Long Caye Ridge

Long Caye Ridge is the third in a series of excellent walls and shallow reefs off the western side of Long Caye. It gets its name from a protruding ridge of reefs that form a small promontory just north of Tres Cocos. Spur-and-groove formations are well defined here on the bottom, leading to the wall and a drop-off of major proportions. The grooves run perpendicular to the wall and feed directly into the open sea.

Typical Depth Range:
  40 ft (12 meters) to unlimited (wall)
Typical Current Conditions: Minimal
Typical Visibility: 80 ft (24 meters)
Expertise Required: Novice

The sponges, coral and fish here are similar to those seen on Hat Caye Drop-off. Near the drop-off and all along the wall are many large and colorful sponges and delicate gorgonians. Beneath the canopy of softcoral, tube and vase sponges are fresh growths of boulder, yellow pencil and finger corals. Deep parts of the wall are shingled with large plates of sheet and sunray coral, along with wire coral and small feather black coral trees. Look among the coral recesses for spotted filefish, arrow blennies, crabs, and lobsters. Threespot and dusky damselfish will charge you if you get too close to their algal gardens along the reef top. This is another stop along the Long Caye wall where your searching will reward you with some great photographic subjects.

F.O. MEYER

A diver checks out giant brain coral along the wall.

14 Que Brada

If you move .5 mile north of Long Caye Ridge you will come to a small reentrant in the reef known as Que Brada or "broken reef." This is another great dive site. Here, a narrow ridge of corals rims a crescent-shaped wall. As elsewhere off the west side of Long Caye, the wall is vertical to slightly overhanging. At about 130 ft, a narrow sandy terrace littered with coral provides the only respite on this plunge to unexplored depths. Most dive boats anchor in one of several large sandy areas that interrupt the otherwise continuous coral growth just south of the reentrant. Divers entering the water will see abundant isolated stacks of coral scattered across the sandy bottom beneath the boat. The coral patches extend right up the wall which, if followed north just a short distance, turns abruptly to the east.

Like elsewhere off Long Caye, coral and sponge growth provide plenty of interesting photography and color, but the

Typical Depth Range:
   40 ft (12 meters) to unlimited (wall)
Typical Current Conditions: Minimal
Typical Visibility: 80 ft (24 meters)
Expertise Required: Novice

most exciting photo subjects are friendly and varied fish. Live-aboard dive boats have been feeding fish here for several years now. Schools of yellowtail snappers shadow divers on the reefs. Large black groupers, ocean triggerfish and a host of others are abundant on the shallow wall and reef crest. Virtually all can be approached and photographed without much difficulty. Large spotted eagle rays and turtles also frequent the wall of this dive site.

Due to a history of fish feeding at Que Brada, divers may find themselves surrounded by yellowtail snappers eager for a handout.

15 Cathedral Reef

Cathedral Reef starts shallow with the wall cresting at 30 ft. Unlike other parts of the Long Caye reef system, those at Cathedral are deeply segmented. Sculptured by and rising above the glistening sand channels are colorful coral spires and formations, which have inspired the name Cathedral. Divers will find exploring the top of the reef a rewarding experience especially when descending among the coral towers. You'll find great narrow passages and short tunnels beside some interesting and different marine life.

Typical Depth Range:
30 ft (9 meters) to unlimited (wall)
Typical Current Conditions: Minimal
Typical Visibility: 50 ft (15 meters)
Expertise Required: Intermediate

Macro photographers will love Cathedral. A lush coral garden adorns the reef top and a collection of sponges paints the deep parts of each coral stack red and orange. Healthy growths of boulder, brain and large plates of cactus coral make excellent photographic subjects. Sea anemones are varied and spread their tentacles out from protective coral nooks. Many act as protective hosts for little spotted brown and Pederson Cleaner shrimps. A varied and friendly fish population adds to the spectacle. Fish watchers will take delight with large French angels, stoplight parrots, trumpets, groupers and schools of yellowtail snappers. The angels and snappers are particularly easy photographic targets.

Beyond the shallow reef, large sheet coral up to 6 ft across mantle the wall. Here, huge basket, rope and long yellow tube sponges add form and grace to the rocky wall. Wire coral, deep-water lace and other soft coral form elegant growths that extend up to 5 ft from the wall. Look for turtles and lobsters among the living cover on the wall. Also keep an eye on the deep parts of the reef below you, and on the open sea, for large pelagics, such as eagle rays and huge groupers or jewfish.

F.O. MEYER

Large sponges and corals are first in line for plankton swept over the reef by currents.

16 Silver Caves

Just north of Cathedral, the reef forms a promontory. The reef here is shallow and deeply segmented. Coral development sets this site apart from all others. Huge coral formations create a framework riddled with cavities that make excellent hiding places for animals trying to escape predators. This dive site's name was inspired by the huge schools of silversides that were found regularly inside the caves. They were a spectacle to behold, but unfortunately, abundant amounts have not been seen in the caves for the past few years.

The absence of silversides does not totally diminish the attractiveness of this dive site. Exciting discoveries can be made here and photographers can have some interesting challenges. Many of the nocturnal or light-sensitive animals can be found here during the daytime. A flashlight will reveal brittle starfish and sea urchins, waiting for sunset in their cave refuge. It will also turn what normally appears as a black hole into a brilliantly colored grotto. Red and orange encrusting sponges and moss animals carpet the sides and ceilings. Some searching among the richly colored surfaces may lead you to discover basket starfish and some rare sponges in shallow water. Bas-

Typical Depth Range:
  40 ft (12 meters) to unlimited (wall)
Typical Current Conditions:
  None to minimal
Typical Visibility: 80 ft (24 meters)
Expertise Required: Intermediate

ket starfish look very different during the day. With their arms wrapped around their round bodies, they form thin, white disks. Cave ceilings are an especially favorite resting place for these animals.

Few people have seen and recognized sclerosponges. In fact, they were considered extinct and were only rediscovered in the last 20 years when diving made studying deep reefs possible. These sponges are important reef builders below 150 ft and are now known to occupy caves in shallow water. Although rare, you can see them at this dive site. Peer into the grottos and look among the red sponges for small mounds of yellow to pale green that have the typical star pattern of the sclerosponges.

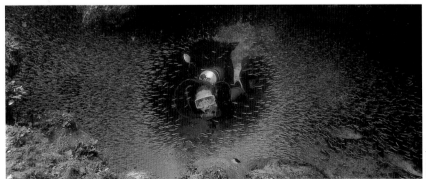

This is the scene at Silver Caves as it used to look, when thousands of silversides inhabited the grottoes.

17 The Aquarium

Off the northwestern corner of Long Caye, the main reef trend turns abruptly to the east. In doing so, it forms a major point and begins a significant change in reef topography. Well-defined, long coral ridges and sandy canyons run perpendicular to the reef line here and farther eastward. These begin shallow, extending seaward to 60 ft or more below the surface. Like Silver Caves, the coral ridges have many holes and grottos, providing a haven for all kinds of invertebrate and fish life.

Typical Depth Range:
  30 ft (9 meters) to unlimited (wall)
Typical Current Conditions:
  Minimal to strong
Typical Visibility: 80 ft (24 meters)
Expertise Required: Intermediate

Moderate to strong currents flow across the reef here almost all the time. They are strongest over the reef top and may be entirely absent along the wall itself. Divers who explore the north-facing wall of the point may find troublesome currents too and are advised to plan their dive accordingly. Currents along the point generally sweep across the reef from the east. To

F.O. MEYER

A cluster of delicate tunicates pumps food from the currents that sweep past the reefs.

minimize the effect of the current, divers should drop down to the reef surface. By swimming east at the start, you will enjoy an effortless return trip to the boat.

Named for its varied invertebrate life, the Aquarium is a good place to see the common and unusual. Crinoids or sea feathers are of special interest here during the day. Many of these animals, which are normally hidden deep in the reef elsewhere, are more visible at the Aquarium. A good place to look for them is near the crest of the wall. Their orange or yellow feather-like arms are fully exposed here. Only the small body and cirri (attach-ment appendages) are tucked beneath the coral formations.

Deep-water lace coral and black coral are other common animals along the top 50 ft of the wall. Most extend horizontally away from the wall with their network of branches oriented perpendicular to the slight current that occasionally sweeps the reef.

Fish are also varied and colorful at this site. If you look on top of the reef and in the dividing channels, you can find the usual variety of tropicals. Parrotfish of all shapes, sizes and varieties graze on the algae patches that mantle much of the reef top.

18 Nurse Shark Lodge

East of the Aquarium, on the same reef, lies Nurse Shark Lodge, a wall that plunges steeply into deep water all along this section of northern Long Caye. It offers great diving, but the site is singled out by dive charters because it constantly features large marine life.

Dive site names are often drawn from physical characteristics of the site or from exciting animal sightings. This site is no exception, regularly offering shark sightings, although I've not seen any during my dives here. The "Lodge" portion of the name refers to shallow caves that riddle the reefs and are reportedly used as sleeping quarters for sharks.

Typical Depth Range:
   40 ft (12 meters) to unlimited (wall)
Typical Current Conditions:
   None to minimal
Typical Visibility: 80 ft (24 meters)
Expertise Required: Intermediate

Why sharks persistently visit here is not known, but elsewhere in the world they are attracted to a particular promontory because of unusually rich feeding conditions. Whatever the reason for their presence here, sharks are a thrilling site for any diver.

Spur-and-groove formations that dominate here are also excellent for photography of corals, sponges and a variety of other invertebrates. Reef fish also like the many nooks, crannies and alleys that make excellent hiding places and predator escape routes.

J. LEEK

Nurse sharks are found resting beneath coral ledges.

19 Eagle Ray Wall

Opposite a tidal cut through the north end of Long Caye and near Nurse Shark Lodge lies Eagle Ray Wall. This area has an excellent shallow reef and colorful wall, exciting and ideal for snorkelers. The reef is no more than 3.5-40 ft beneath the surface right up to the wall. A series of long, straight coral ridges separated by sand gullies serve as natural navigation aids. Snorkelers following these structures into shallow water are led straight to the reef crest, whereas divers are directed to the wall in the opposite direction.

The wall plunges dramatically into deep water all along this part of the reef trend, where it is rich with corals and colorful red cup sponges. Here too, many painted tunicates occur clustered on a variety of soft coral branches between 60-65 ft deep. This wall is also riddled with many holes and grottos, which are home to a variety of fish and invertebrates.

On most dives here you can see eagle rays in graceful flight just off the wall. Usually, these magnificent creatures are seen about 40 ft below the surface, moving effortlessly through the water with majestic, slow sweeps of their wings. Their regular occurrence here may enable you to plan for some spectacular photographs or video with much depth of field.

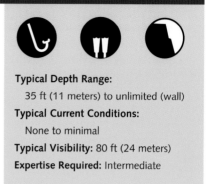

Typical Depth Range:
   35 ft (11 meters) to unlimited (wall)
Typical Current Conditions:
   None to minimal
Typical Visibility: 80 ft (24 meters)
Expertise Required: Intermediate

Even if rays don't happen by, there are still plenty of photographic opportunities. Boats anchored here will sometimes swing parallel to the wall, making excellent silhouette shots with lots of colorful foreground.

Spotted eagle rays cruise in open water just off the wall.

A diver explores the coral ridge that is home to a variety of invertebrates.

20 Southwest Cut

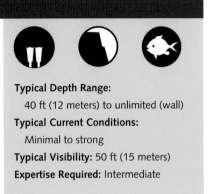

Bordered by a wide channel, this site is exposed to a flood of lagoon water and sometimes ocean swells that cross the lagoon from the windward side. Frequent changes in current strength, visibility and water temperature can be expected during the day, except when winds come from the north or northwest. Even when favorable winds exist, water temperature will change dramatically near the wall, where a plume of warm lagoon water escapes in the channel, crosses the reef and passes over the cool water of the open sea.

Typical Depth Range:
  40 ft (12 meters) to unlimited (wall)
Typical Current Conditions:
  Minimal to strong
Typical Visibility: 50 ft (15 meters)
Expertise Required: Intermediate

The reef at Southwest Cut is peculiar. Much of the reef top is covered with algae, soft coral and sand. The reef is dissected by wide sand channels that plunge steeply to great depths. Except for local accumulations of turtle grass mats, the channels are pretty much barren of marine life. Only the wall with its many grottos and holes appears to team with life and offers the best opportunity to see shrimp, eels and various other organisms.

The variety of marine life seen during the day at this site can take your breath

J. BUREK

A steady diet of zoanthid polyps keeps the gills of a nudibranch armed with stinging cells.

away, but the most consistent good diving occurs here at night. Dozens of basket starfish can be seen clinging to soft corals near and on the wall. A varied collection of eels also emerge from their shelters in the reef. Many come to the turtle grass mats in the channel to feed, while others, such as sharptail eels, are most frequently spotted in the large coral heads behind the wall. Here and elsewhere on the sand flats or among the scattered coral heads are good places to find scorpion fish and loads of tarpons can be seen swimming above the reef. You might also see some unusual critters here, such as the yellow-banded coral shrimp or the sail-finned blenny. You can also get right up to some of the trunkfish and filefish for some excellent photographs. Huge hogfish congregate here too, and there are always some nudibranchs or manta rays to spice up the diving at this site.

21 West Point I & II

Along the northern limb of Lighthouse are two infrequently visited dive sites. The southernmost is called West Point I, with West Point II to the north. Both have excellent diving, but visibility can drop to 50 ft or less when the winds blow steadily out of the east or northeast. But the poor visibility is normally limited to the upper 20 ft.

Both reefs have a narrow rim adjacent to a wall that plunges to 125 ft. The wall is vertical to slightly overhanging

Typical Depth Range:
  25 ft (8 meters) to unlimited (wall)
Typical Current Conditions:
  Slight to moderate
Typical Visibility: 50 ft (15 meters)
Expertise Required: Novice

RICK TEGLER

Angelfish are frequent visitors to the West Point.

in most places. A variety of sponges and corals decorate the wall with many shapes and colors. Below 125 ft there is a narrow terrace covered with sand and a sparse cover of coral. The gently sloped terrace leads right up to the edge of a second deep wall.

If watching or photographing fish is on your list, this is the one place you don't want to miss. Schools of smooth trunkfish, all four angelfish (queen, gray, French and rock beauty) and lots of parrotfish congregate here. Yellowtail snappers appear in great numbers, along with queen trigger-

fish, white spotted filefish, hogfish, barracudas and tiger groupers. All the butterflyfish feed on the reef here too, including the rare longsnout. A variety of creole wrasses, blennies, gobies and hamlets need to also be included on this partial list.

Even if fish are not your main interest, you will find this site a joy to dive. Here too, the coral is healthy and at least as varied as the fish life. Conch and garden eels are found in the sand slopes behind the reef wall, whereas spotted and green moray eels hide in healthy coral growths.

22 Half Moon Wall

Half Moon Wall is an exceptional dive site now included in the newly erected Half Moon Caye National Monument on Lighthouse. Anyone who has the opportunity to dive the offshore atolls should try to dive Half Moon Wall. Here, you can make several different types of dives without moving the boat, and between dives you can take time to picnic or observe the boobie bird colony on Half Moon Caye. It is one of my favorite dives because the reefs are so spectacular and varied.

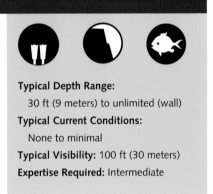

Typical Depth Range:
  30 ft (9 meters) to unlimited (wall)
Typical Current Conditions:
  None to minimal
Typical Visibility: 100 ft (30 meters)
Expertise Required: Intermediate

The beauty of Half Moon Caye is now protected.

J. CONKLIN

Located on the south side of Half Moon Caye are two striking reef features. First, the coral formations form a narrow rim at the edge of the wall which, in most places, is only 100-200 ft wide. Second, an extensive gently sloping, seemingly barren sand flat separates the reef rim from shallow reefs along the shore.

As you glide down to the reefs 30 ft below, you will see the reef rim has a spectacular development of spurs and grooves. The living spurs are massive coral accumulations subdivided by seaward sloping grooves up to 30 ft deep at the wall. Many grooves are quite narrow, but easily negotiated by a diver. One of the exciting aspects of this dive is entering one of the grooves and following it seaward. Muddy sand floors the grooves and divers should take special precautions not to stir up the bottom with their fins. Many grooves feature pronounced overhangs that locally coalesce to form tunnels, also known as Grover's Grottos. All tunnels are short and straight so no special dive equipment or experience is needed. As the tunnels near the wall they reach depths of 70 ft or more.

Large and small marine life abounds on the Half Moon Wall reefs. It is extremely varied because of the abrupt and extensive change in bottom type. If you want to see garden eels, conch, rays, flounder, star-eye hermit crabs and tilefish, check out the sand flats behind the reefs rimming the wall. Manta rays and a variety of reef fish forage in this area regularly, too.

On the reef, groupers and yellowtail snappers hide out beneath the coral hanging over the reef canyons. Razorfish and toadfish are another common sight on the reef, adjacent to the sloping sand flat. Large pelagics frequent the reef wall. Spotted eagle rays and turtles are most common, but occasionally sharks and large black groupers visit the area. Most of the large marine life is found more frequently along the eastern part of this dive site, as the large pelagics venture in from the open sea to the east.

All divers should take time to see the spectacular field of garden eels found on the sloping sand flats behind the reefs along the wall. Thousands of eels can be seen from a distance off the western end of Half Moon Caye. But you will only see their graceful, slender bodies protruding from a hole in the sand from a distance. These animals are extremely shy and

getting a close look may take considerable time. As you approach them you will see successive waves of eels retreat into their protective sand flat shelters.

Bird Watching on Half Moon Caye

Located within the Lighthouse Reef atoll less than 10 ft above sea level is the Half Moon Caye Natural Monument. These 45 acres of protected bird sanctuary are home to two distinct ecosystems: to the west, the lush vegetation is fertilized by the droppings of thousands of seabirds, including some 4,000 endangered red-footed boobies (the wonderfully named, magnificent frigatebird) and 98 other species of birds. To the east, there is less vegetation but more coconut palms. Endangered loggerhead and hawksbill turtles lay their eggs on the southern beaches. There are no accommodations, but camping is allowed in some areas and organized boat trips make a point of stopping at this bird lovers' haven.

KEVIN SCHAFER

The red-footed booby bird.

23 Blue Hole

The origin of Blue Hole dates back to an ice age about 15,000 years ago. Enough sea water was frozen in glaciers during this time to lower sea level more than 350 ft, exposing the limestones of Lighthouse Reef. Huge subterranean caverns formed when fresh water flowed through the limestone deposits. Since then, the roof of the cavern has collapsed to form the sinkhole.

Made famous by a Jacques Cousteau's 1970 *Calypso* expedition, Blue Hole is one of the best known dive sites in Belize. It is a circular, deep depression in the center of more than 75 sq miles of shallow, blue-green water. Its diameter at the rim measures 1,045 ft, whereas its maximum depth is 412 ft. Except for two narrow passages on the eastern and northern rims, Blue Hole is completely rimmed by living coral.

For the advanced diver this site is well worth the trip. You should plan to dive either the north or south side to a depth of 100-150 ft where the shallowest cave

Typical Depth Range:
5-412 ft (2 to 126 meters) to
unlimited (wall)
Typical Current Conditions: None
Typical Visibility: 100 ft (30 meters)
Expertise Required: Advanced

features are found. Begin your dive by snorkeling to the coral rim. This serves two purposes: first, it conserves air, and second, it provides an opportunity to get everyone making the dive together before you descend. Your no-decompression bottom time is short at the planned depths so it is best to snorkel toward the center to Blue Hole, just beyond the vertical wall, before descending.

A good way of maintaining your orientation during descent is to stay reason-

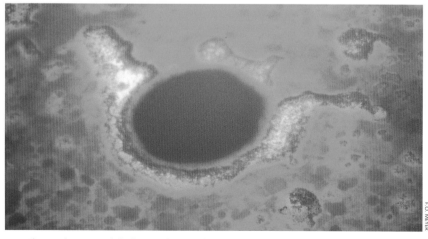

F.O. MEYER

The combination of shallow reef and deep water makes the Blue Hole great for both diving and snorkeling.

J. LEEK

Large stalactities in a dimly lit cavern are sculptured by thousands of years of geological change.

ably close to the wall. As you descend, you will notice that the wall crests between 40-55 ft and continues as a vertical cliff to a depth of 90-100 ft before receding at a 55° angle. The resulting overhang forms a cavern ceiling from which hang stalactites more than 3 ft in diameter and up to 20 ft in length. Also found adorning the ceiling are numerous dripstone pillows. More than 50 ft below the crest of the ceiling, the cave floor is riddled with a collection of fallen stalactites, muddy sediment and an opening to a cave system. Surprisingly, the dimly lit walls of the cavern are covered by a variety of filamentous green algae, boring sponges and encrusting worms. Little other marine life appears present in the cavern, but the walls above are covered with cornflake algae and isolated growths of gorgonians. Sharks and turtles may be found here, but their presence in Blue Hole is unpredictable.

Marine life in Blue Hole and on the broad muddy sand slope that surrounds it is rather dismal, comparitive to other sites in Belize. Algae and encrusting sponges mantle the walls to depth. Scattered growths of unhealthy stony coral rim the wall and occur scattered across the broad, muddy sand slope between the wall and shallow reefs. Most corals are heavily encrusted by red algae, hydroids and gorgonians. The only other conspicuous organisms here are shaving brush and mermaid's fan algae.

The most varied and lush marine life is found on the coral reefs that rim the perimeter of Blue Hole. The reefs occur in only a few feet of water, making them excellent for snorkeling. Stands of elkhorn, club finger and shallow-water starlet corals, giant green anemones and arious urchins occupy the shallow lagoon habitat.

Glover's Reef Dive Sites

Named for pirate John Glover, Glover's Reef is the most southern of the three offshore reef systems and features some spectacular dive sites. Glover's distance from Belize City and Ambergris makes it a less frequently visited destination. Many of the islands in the southern part of Belize are virtually uncharted virgin territory, so southerly dive trips take a little more planning and creative organizing, but are well worth the effort. Those divers up for the adventure will find all the reefs along the atoll's southeastern limb feature dive sites abounding with shallow walls, fresh reefs and abundant pelagics.

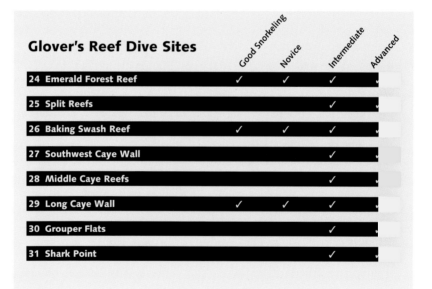

Glover's Reef Dive Sites	Good Snorkeling	Novice	Intermediate	Advanced
24 Emerald Forest Reef	✓	✓	✓	✓
25 Split Reefs			✓	✓
26 Baking Swash Reef	✓	✓	✓	✓
27 Southwest Caye Wall			✓	✓
28 Middle Caye Reefs			✓	✓
29 Long Caye Wall	✓	✓	✓	✓
30 Grouper Flats			✓	✓
31 Shark Point			✓	✓

Glover's Reef

0   2   4 km

0   1   2 miles

not for navigation

87° 45' W

31

North
Caye

24

25

30

26

Northeast
Caye

Long
Caye

29

Middle
Caye

28

Southwest
Cayes

27

16° 45' N

CARIBBEAN
SEA

87° 45' W

Depth

Reef

0 - 16.5 feet

16.5 - 160.5 feet

160.5+ feet

24 Emerald Forest Reef

Emerald Forest Reef is a new dive site along a stretch of virgin reef that forms Glover's western limb. It is located about 7 miles from both the light on Glover's northeast end, and from the northern-most group of cayes on the atoll's east side. Here, the reef slopes uniformly to the west from its crest to a sloping wall. The water is only 1 ft deep above the reef crest and no more than 50 ft below the surface near the wall. The shallow water, lack of currents and marvelous fresh reef make this site an excellent place for new divers or those who have been away from diving for some time. Even snorkelers will find this an excellent spot because the most luxurious and active reef is no more than 25 ft below the surface. Experienced divers will find

Typical Depth Range:
  15-70 ft (5-21 meters)
Typical Current Conditions: None
Typical Visibility: 50 ft (15 meters)
Expertise Required: Novice

Emerald Forest equally rewarding, both in the shallows and on the wall.

Emerald Forest is named for its huge elkhorn coral that dominates the reef crest in shallow water. Impressive growths of this coral feature trunks more than 1 ft in diameter and a canopy of branches 10 ft above the reef surface. When the sea is

Magnificent, huge elkhorn coral dominate the reef crest of Emerald Forest.

calm look for crabs, reef urchins, brittle starfish and boring sponges among the stands of huge coral.

Just a short distance seaward from the elkhorn stand is an absolutely luxurious coral garden every photographer will want to visit. Every variety of stony coral known to live in shallow water can be photographed in this one area. All are healthy and the dense growth of coral life provides ample shelter for many snappers, groupers, trunkfish and angels. Wrasses and blue chromis are especially abundant.

Divers should also explore the reef along and on the wall. The terrain near the wall is a series of weakly developed coral ridges and shallow sandy gullies. On the ridges sit a fine collection of club finger coral, large brain coral, yellow pencil coral, the ever-present boulder coral and lots of forked sea feathers. This growth of animals houses numerous gobie and shrimp cleaning stations for groupers, bar jacks and parrotfish.

The wall is a good place to look for large lobsters among shingled and platy growths of boulder and sheet coral. There are also large basket, tube, rope sponges and a wide variety of small marine life, all of which make interesting photo subjects.

25 Split Reefs

Named for its characteristic reef development, this dive site features a profile with two distinct reef zones over a distance of about 800 ft. A shallow reef extends from sea level to 40 ft and a deeper reef begins at 70 ft, extending to more than 100 ft at the wall. Between them is a sloping sand flat with a few scattered growths of stony and soft corals.

The shallow reef is a photographer's and videographer's delight. A healthy, colorful and varied growth of corals makes this an ideal place for coral close-ups. Magnificent stands of elkhorn, meandrine brain, large cactus, thin fungus and staghorn coral form crowded coral stands. Colorful sea whips, sea rods, corky sea fingers and Venus sea fans also grace the reef. Movement and additional color are provided

Typical Depth Range:
40-100 ft (12-30 meters)
Typical Current Conditions: None
Typical Visibility: 50 ft (15 meters)
Expertise Required: Intermediate

F. BUREK

Soft corals, like trees on land, create lofty perches for many other organisms.

F.O. MEYER

A prominent formation of pillar coral provides shelter for this black grouper.

by crowds of blue chromis, sergeant majors and blue-headed wrasse that glide over and through the corals. By looking beneath the coral canopy and into some of the countless nooks that riddle the reef, you can find additional tropicals and abundant, brilliantly colored sponges. Because the reef is more than 300 ft wide, a virtually unlimited number of reef organisms can be found. Best of all, you can stay here a long time because most of the reef is less than 30 ft deep.

If you are more impressed by size than variation in marine life, the deep reef is for you. Beginning at depths of 70 ft, a mountainous coral mesa towers as much as 50 ft above the sloping sand flats leading to the wall. Much of the deep reef is built by boulder, lettuce and large-cupped boulder coral and adorned by a variety of deep-water sea whips and rods. An interesting ecological adaptation to low light that you can look for on the deep reef is the development of skirts or platy growths among the boulder corals.

26 Baking Swash Reef

Baking Swash is a narrow cut through the western limb of Glover's atoll. Two weathered tree limbs mark the channel on each side. The cut through the reef is wide and deep enough to accommodate only small, manageable boats with a shallow draft. It is lined with coral and no more than 10 ft deep. Although shallow, narrow and remote, the channel itself can be a dangerous place to dive. Wave and tidal currents are not a problem, but power boats from local resorts use this passage because it is the only cut in the western limb of the atoll. Most captains are familiar with the cut and speed through it with little expectation of divers.

Typical Depth Range:
  15-100 ft (5-30 meters)
Typical Current Conditions: None
Typical Visibility: 70 ft (21 meters)
Expertise Required: Novice

Reef development occurs over a broad, sloping bottom in two zones separated by a sand flat. The shallow reefs grow up to sea level on either side of Baking Swash channel and extend 30 ft below the sea surface.

The deep reefs are seaward of a wide sand flat that features only a sparse cover of corals. Huge towers of coral form impressive mounds with up to 50 ft (15 meters) of relief.

Considerable variation exists in the marine life found on the two reef zones. Deep reefs are dominated by huge large-cup boulder coral and elegant growths of deep water lace coral. They are usually not nearly as varied and spectacular as the shallow reefs, so unless you simply want to do a deep dive, it is best to stay on the shallow reefs. Because the visibility is low, macrophotography is probably the best here. Corals are very healthy and varied with most of the Caribbean species of hard and soft corals present.

With reef space at a premium, club finger and shallow-water starlet corals compete for space.

A diver explores the shallow reef structures off Glover's Reef.

27 Southwest Caye Wall

Squarely off Southwest Caye's east side and only a short distance from the Manta Resort Pier, you'll find a sloping reef and wall that offer consistently good diving. Both are part of a narrow reef line that forms the southeastern limb of Glover's Reef. Depth increases rapidly away from the reef crest before deepening more gradually a short distance from the wall. Overall the reef has little topography, uneven only near the wall. Here, wedge-shaped coral ridges are separated by wide, shallow sand channels. While doing a safety stop at 10 ft, divers will see all coral wedges border and point away from the wall.

Like many walls on the windward limbs of the atolls, the Southwest Caye Wall is a dramatic drop-off. From its crest at 50 ft, this underwater cliff plunges to 130 ft. A narrow shelf floored by platy boulder coral, a tangle of wire coral and an abundance of sand occur at this depth. From

Typical Depth Range:
   50 (15 meters) to unlimited
Typical Current Conditions:
   Minimal to none
Typical Visibility: 90 ft (28 meters)
Expertise Required: Intermediate

there, the wall resumes its vertical descent to more than 350 ft before changing to a steep slope. Submarine dives made here show invertebrate growth is sparse at these depths.

Shallow parts of the wall have either giant overhangs or are deeply furrowed. Graceful gorgonians, wire coral and some very attractive and photogenic sponges adorn the overhangs, which are ideally suited for pictures with dramatic and colorful compositions. Divers taking pictures beneath an overhang need to remember to plan their pictures in advance so they can avoid lots of breathing while under the overhangs. Otherwise, exhaled bubbles will dislodge enough sediment to make good photography impossible.

Wall diving is an exhilarating experience, but it also means deep diving at Southwest Caye Wall. Unlike some drop-offs elsewhere on these atolls, this one begins at a modest depth and does not allow divers to work their way up to a shallow reef. Check your time and depth frequently and allow plenty of time for your ascent. This way you should have plenty of air left for a slow ascent and a three-minute safety stop at 10 ft.

H. PARKEY
A sea feather makes an ideal nighttime hang-out.

Divers find the luxuriant sponge growth a compelling attraction on the precipitous wall off Southwest Caye.

28 Middle Caye Reefs

Located about a third of the way up on the windward southeastern reefs, Middle Caye Reefs is one of the most remote dive sites on Glover's Reef. The site derives its name from the small palm and mangrove covered caye developed behind the reef crest.

Many of the dive boats visit this reef, but it is usually a charter rather than a regularly scheduled run. If you want to dive this area, it is best to check with various live-aboards to determine when they intend to go there, or arrange for a trip to Manta Resort on Southwest Cayes at the extreme southern end of Glover's Reef. Even if you manage to arrange a trip, exceptional conditions are required to actually make the dive. Calm or westerly winds are needed to keep boats from swinging over and crashing into the shallow coral growths of this narrow reef

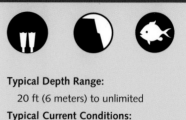

Typical Depth Range:
   20 ft (6 meters) to unlimited
Typical Current Conditions:
   Minimal to none
Typical Visibility: 100 ft (30 meters)
Expertise Required: Intermediate

tract. Another problem is large, incoming swells, which are common while storms are blowing in the Gulf and Caribbean. These can make getting back into your dive boat too dangerous for safe diving. But if the conditions are right, this site is well worth it.

F. BUREK

By day, juvenile basket starfish stay hidden deep in the reef, but at night they climb onto sea fans to feed.

DAVID SAILORS

Invertebrates, like this spiny lobster, thrive in the coral at Middle Caye Reefs.

Middle Caye Reefs offer some exceptional diving opportunities. A large variety of reef organisms can be found in a limited area because reef zones are condensed on the narrow fore reef. The entire area between the reef crest and wall is only several hundred yards wide. Reef formations are lush and healthy in this zone, with few areas overgrown by fleshy algae. The wall, which crests at 40 ft here, is spectacular and richly adorned with reef organisms. It also differs from wall profiles seen at most other locations because it is terraced at depth. Clear water and minimal currents allow you to see at least two terraces without making a dive below 100 ft. The first terrace at 150 ft and the second terrace at 210 ft are seaward-sloping surfaces covered by platy boulder coral. Coral coverage is thorough and gives these terraces the appearance of a shingled roof.

Virtually every kind of invertebrate and a wide variety of fish can be found at Middle Caye. Turtle grass beds with their unique collection of tiny organisms flourish in patches adjacent to the northern and southern shores. Small foraminifera, encrusting red algae and hydrozoans cling to the blades of these grasses, whereas several kinds of clams seek shelter among the plant roots. Turban snails abound in the rocky areas bordering the island. Here large heads of common smooth star, smooth and depressed brain corals and yellow porous coral form isolated growths that are surrounded by coral rubble, much of which is coated with red algae. Exceptional growths of tan lettuce-leaf create shallow coral spurs at 10 ft. Reef urchins, red boring sponges, and many other kinds of organisms hide or live on these large elongated coral growths.

By far the greatest diversity of marine life exists near the drop-off. You'll find some less common stony corals such as meandrine brain, rare rose, giant brain, large flower and large cactus corals. Forked sea feathers, knobby candelabra, deadman's fingers and common bushy soft corals sway elegantly on the reef surface. Red finger, lavender tube, giant tube and variable sponges decorate the reef with their brilliant colors and create homes for thousands of small shrimp, crabs and fish. The orange sea lily is especially common here. Densities of 25 individuals are not uncommon.

Orange crinoids are abundant along the shallow wall at Middle Caye.

29 Long Caye Wall

Long Caye Wall offers more than just wall diving. Just off its eastern shore is a shallow reef and snorkelers or divers can enter from the beach. Getting in is a bit rough and a beach entry is not advisable on days with large swells or heavy seas. Fire coral and elkhorn coral grow in great profusion close to shore, but there are some openings in the coral. On good days, look for openings among the dense coral growth before getting in the water. Once you get past this initial barrier, the snorkel or dive is easy. A large variety of stony and soft corals flourish on this shallow reef. Many of the corals grow in less than 20 ft of water, so snorkelers can see everything.

Typical Depth Range:
30 ft (9 meters) to unlimited
Typical Current Conditions: None
Typical Visibility: 90 ft (28 meters)
Expertise Required: Novice

Farther seaward, divers reach a sand and coral rubble zone. The coral rubble is part of a gradual transition from coral reef to a broad sand slope. Between 20-30 ft, the belt is mostly a barren blanket of

J. LEEK

Yellowhead jawfish, like this one posturing near its burrow, are one of several attractions found on the sand and eel grass flats behind the coral rim at Long Caye.

rippled sand. Its only residents are sand divers and jawfish, which disappear into sand or burrows when approached.

Sand ripples die out below 30 ft, but the sand belt continues to trail off to 45 ft before ending abruptly at the base of a reef ridge. The sand is marked with burrows, feeding marks and a variety of animal trails.

Garden eels are one of several permanent residents. A small group of these shy creatures lives in burrows close to the area of sand waves. Other invertebrates here are alpheid shrimp and various mollusks. All live in the soft sands and are rarely found during the day except by visiting rays or other fish actively rooting for them.

Reaching within 35 ft of the surface, the wall is an exciting experience found 700 ft squarely off Long Caye. Seasoned divers soaring over the wall can explore a vertical drop with many overhangs. The wall is mantled with giant plates of sheet and boulder coral below 50 ft. Colorful sponges, wire coral, black coral and many hydroids are most abundant on deep parts of the wall. Every kind of soft coral imaginable forms a dense forest on shallow wall and its crest. Divers who prefer to watch for large animals will not be disappointed here either. Turtles, eagle rays, manta rays and barracudas are regular visitors all along the wall. This drop-off can provide you with many thrilling dives.

BARRY OPPEN

A diver checks out a cluster of yellow tube sponge.

30 Grouper Flats

Another site standing out along the north-eastern reef tract, Grouper Flats consists of lens-shaped reefs similar to those at Shark Point. It is a gently sloping reef of little relief and home to a large variety of groupers. It has two types of reefs, a shallow reef that extends to 30 ft and a very wide, deep reef beginning at 40 ft and extending to 80 ft. The shallow reef features mature elkhorn and huge masses

Typical Depth Range:
40-60 ft (12-18 meters)
Typical Current Conditions: None
Typical Visibility: 70 ft (21 meters)
Expertise Required: Intermediate

of lettuce coral that look like loaves of bread densely covered with a growth of lettuce leaves. These shallow coral

S. MEYER

Nassau grouper willingly pose for portraits.

Tiger grouper

ing and coalescing rivers of white sand. Although the reef has little relief, it is riddled with holes and crevices.

Grouper Flats got its name, naturally, from the many groupers that inhabit the gentle topography of the deep reef. They seek shelter within a virtual forest of soft coral and the endless number of crevices in the stony coral growths. Nassau, tiger, black, spotted and marble grouper are seen lying amid the sea whips and sea feathers. They are especially abundant and varied in the shallow part of the deep reef.

formations are replaced by lens-shaped reef masses that are subdivided by wind-

31 Shark Point

Located at the eastern end of the windward northern reefs, Shark Point is one of the more remote dive sites on Glover's. Heavy seas generally pound this exposed stretch of reef, making it a difficult site.

Distance and weather play a major role in determining if you can dive. The nearest resort equipped with day boats is nearly 9 miles away from Shark Point. Even if divers are willing to make the hour-long trip to get there, prolonged periods of

Typical Depth Range:
  50-90 ft (15-27 meters)
Typical Current Conditions:
  None to heavy
Typical Visibility: 100 ft (30 meters)
Expertise Required: Intermediate

Hammerhead sharks have impressive, powerful bodies, accentuated by flattened heads.

excessive boat roll can make for an unset-tling experience. Heavy seas create extreme boat motion and increase the risk of injury to divers exiting the water on day boats or live-aboards. Experienced divers may visit this site using Zodiacs launched from a larger vessel anchored inside the lagoon. These small rubberized crafts can quickly and safely transport divers to and from the reef, in fair weather.

When weather and sea conditions allow access to the reef point, the diving is sen-sational. A wide variety of sharks, seen almost always on these reefs, offer a unique and exhilarating experience. Nurse, black-tip, hammerhead and tiger sharks can all be seen together here on the sand channels and coral hills. attracted to this part of the re tain, but it may be because th point is one of the premier s ng grounds for groupers and other fish.

Huge, lens-shaped reefs are sculptured by the constant pounding of heavy seas on the gently sloping point down to a depth of 90 ft. Below 20 ft, they are made up of a mixed collection of small living coral colonies and stacks of coral debris. Riddled with holes and spread across a reef more than 1 mile wide, the coral mounds con-tain millions of hiding places for a dazzling array of tropicals.

Turneffe Atoll Dive Sites

Closest to Belize City and easily accessible, Turneffe features spectacular diving suitable for every level of diver. Along the western reef line north of the Elbow, novice divers can feel comfortable on shallow reefs, removed from the steep and deep walls so typical elsewhere. A varied terrain, wrecks and an abundance of marine life make the eastern reefs on Turneffe's southern end sensational for seasoned divers. Current and walls make the diving here challenging but great for finding large pelagics.

Turneffe is the largest of the three atolls and the only one with an extensive cover of mangroves. Most established dive sites are limited to the southern end, but there is enough here for several weeks of diving.

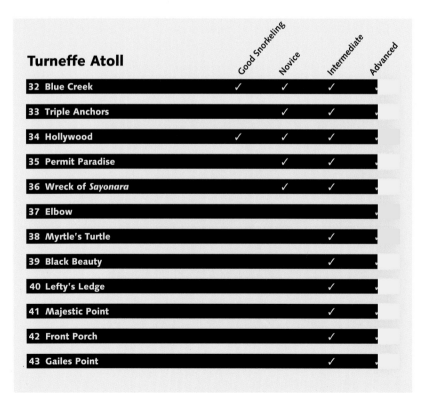

Turneffe Atoll	Good Snorkeling	Novice	Intermediate	Advanced
32 Blue Creek	✓	✓	✓	✓
33 Triple Anchors		✓	✓	✓
34 Hollywood	✓	✓	✓	✓
35 Permit Paradise		✓	✓	✓
36 Wreck of *Sayonara*		✓	✓	✓
37 Elbow				✓
38 Myrtle's Turtle			✓	✓
39 Black Beauty			✓	✓
40 Lefty's Ledge			✓	✓
41 Majestic Point			✓	✓
42 Front Porch			✓	✓
43 Gailes Point			✓	✓

32 Blue Creek

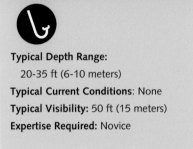

Typical Depth Range:
   20-35 ft (6-10 meters)
Typical Current Conditions: None
Typical Visibility: 50 ft (15 meters)
Expertise Required: Novice

Blue Creek reef is named after the tidal pass that divides a tangle of mangroves a distance behind the western reef line. The reefs at Blue Creek are shallow, broken and have abundant and varied marine life. Snorkelers and less experienced divers will find this site very attractive. Live-aboards visiting this site frequently spend the night here and offer this site as a night dive.

Much of the marine life at Blue Creek is seen only on night dives. Crabs and lobsters are among the most exciting and interesting nocturnal creatures. Although these arthropods generally forage as individuals, dozens of animals can be found searching for food on the sand flats or coral formations after dark, including spectacular giant spider crabs. If you wish to photograph these invertebrates, you will need a wide-angle lens because their bodies alone are too big for a close-up kit framer.

Decorator crabs aren't as large, but they are plentiful, colorful and also active at night. These strange-looking crabs attach a variety of sponges to their bodies, so no two look alike. Look for them on sea fans and sea rods and keep an eye open for large Spanish lobsters. These bizarre creatures like to scrounge for tiny bits of food and are most commonly seen on sand channel floors.

Other invertebrates seen here and best photographed at night include brittle starfish and urchins. Ruby, slimy and Oersted's brittle stars can be found near the entrance of every little reef hole, along with Suenson's brittle stars draped over sponges. You will also find an abundance of reef and long-spined black urchins, both of which shun light and do not wander far from shelter even at night. Although only invertebrates are mentioned here, fish watchers will not be disappointed. Blue Creek makes an exciting dive that everyone can enjoy.

Giant agelus sponges form clusters on coral stacks.

Spider crabs are active at night.

33 Triple Anchors

Triple Anchors is just south along the western reef line from Blue Creek. Its bottom topography and coral formations are typical of this side of Turneffe Atoll, with coral stacks scattered across a broad, gently sloping reef.

Among the coral are scattered remnants of an early 18th century vessel, including a few artifacts and three anchors, which give the site its name. The three anchors occur along a NW/SE line over a distance of several hundred yards. Two large anchors are cemented into the reef in an upright position and a smaller one lies in the sand among the coral formations. It takes an experienced eye to recognize these relics because they are now heavily encrusted with corals and sponges. One of the two large anchors is easily found because it sits a short distance northwest of the mooring system recently installed at the site. Its flukes are completely buried by coral and sponge growths, but its shaft cannot be mistaken, despite the heavy invertebrate encrustations.

The other two anchors can be found in opposite directions. To the northwest is the smaller anchor, whose symmetric form is preserved by the coral. It and the mid-sized anchor are not the best photographic subjects compared to the large anchor southeast of the mooring. Its flukes and shaft remain distinctive.

This dive also has plenty of other attractions. The fish and invertebrate life are varied and provide good

Typical Depth Range:
40-60 ft (12-18 meters)
Typical Current Conditions:
None to minimal
Typical Visibility: 60 ft (18 meters)
Expertise Required: Novice

photographic opportunities. Although there are plenty of large sponges and invertebrate groupings, the visibility is better for close-up or macrophotography. Queen angelfish are particularly impressive subjects here. Three and four of these colorful tropicals can be seen chasing one another among the coral formations. Most are good size, some of the largest I've seen anywhere in the Caribbean, with a length close to 1.5 ft.

J. BUREK

A spiny brittle star and colonial zoanthids rest on a lavender vase sponge.

34 Hollywood

For less experienced or infrequent divers, Hollywood is a good place to get comfortable diving the offshore atolls. Located on the leeward side of Turneffe Islands, this site is sheltered from swells and large waves. The reef here is wide, slopes gently and provides ample shallow-water diving. Dive boats generally anchor in 40-45 ft of water. It takes a good swim seaward to reach water depths greater than 50 ft.

Snorkelers will find they too can enjoy the protected shallows of Hollywood. A swim toward the distant mangroves takes you toward a reef crest that is typically under several feet of water. Because the

Typical Depth Range:
  20-50 ft (6-15 meters)
Typical Current Conditions: None
Typical Visibility: 50 ft (15 meters)
Expertise Required: Novice

reefs are submerged and waves attenuated, this is one of the best places to snorkel the reef crest.

Perhaps the least desirable aspect of this dive site is its low visibility. Although

J. BUREK

Coral and sponge growths are particularly photogenic at Hollywood.

F.O. MEYER

Two mustard hill corals compete for space with an orange sponge.

the water is by no means murky, clouds of suspended matter derived from the atoll are typical. Photographers and snorkelers may find this annoying because reefs at 20-50 ft are lush and varied.

Bathed in turbid waters, the luxuriance of stony and soft corals is surprisingly good. Here the broken reefs are built primarily by abundant tan lettuce leaf and boulder coral. But flower, giant brain, smooth brain and club finger corals also commonly compete for space. Less common are grooved fungus, large cactus, rare rose, large cupped boulder and polygonal corals.

Interspersed among stony corals is an abundance of large soft corals and sponges. Soft corals such as forked sea feathers, sea feathers and sea fans form a virtual forest, reaching 4-5 ft in height and growing on both reef formations and on the sandy floors between the coral build-ups.

Equally impressive is the presence of so many large emergent sponges. Iridescent tube, giant yellow tube, huge vase and basket sponges are common primarily because their survival during storms is enhanced by reduced water turbulence on these shallow, protected reefs.

A large amount of algae garnishes these reefs and supports a varied marine life. These algae are important food sources for a variety of herbivorous fish and urchins. You should take time to look for some filamentous green algal lawns because these are fastidiously weeded and aggressively defended by a variety of damselfish. Most common are the threespot and dusky damselfish, which fend off foraging striped parrotfish and divers with aggressive attacks. Many of the common reef tropicals such as barracudas, trumpet, queen angels, grunts and snappers are sure to be seen.

35 Permit Paradise

Located along the same reef trend, Permit Paradise reefs are similar to those found a short distance north at Hollywood. Looking down from the surface after entering the water, you can see abundant clusters of large coral stacks. Most have 10-15 ft of relief above the white sandy bottom at a depth of 40-60 ft.

Typical Depth Range:
 35-60 ft (11-18 meters)
Typical Current Conditions:
 None to minimal
Typical Visibility: 60 ft (18 meters)
Expertise Required: Novice

Large, deep-bodied permits are present in mid-water above the reef consistently enough for this site to bear their name. These graceful and fast swimming fish feed in small schools and make a challenging photographic subject.

The coral growth is fresh and varied. Forked sea feathers are especially noticeable because they form a virtual forest of swaying branches. Other soft corals contributing to the graceful canopy above a garden of stony coral include corky sea fingers, deep-water lace corals, candelabra and scattered growths of black coral.

Boulder and brain coral form the framework of most coral stacks, but large plates of various kinds of fungus coral are common along with flower and finger corals. Invertebrates and fish of all types find these ideal hiding places, so divers can discover dozens of organisms by exploring a single coral stack.

Adding to the spectacle of color and form are a variety of emergent sponges. Plenty of large basket, yellow tube, rope, iridescent tube and stinking vase sponges rise above to compete for living space with corals. The space struggle is equally great below where encrusting sponges and moss animals monopolize the undersides of corals and line the walls of caverns and reef overhangs.

Stinking vase sponges are shunned by marine predators because they stink when damaged.

36 Wreck of *Sayonara*

Sunk by Dave Bennett in 1985, the *Sayonara* is a modern derelict. It is a former passenger/cargo boat and makes an excellent dive for inexperienced wreck divers. The wreck rests on a bed of coral and sand at a depth of 50 ft, listing slightly to starboard. It has about 15 ft of relief and is intact from fore to aft. Her wooden frame is deteriorating rapidly so entry of the cabin is not advisable as the whole structure may break apart. Besides, she was stripped of everything except the shaft and prop prior to sinking. Exterior exploration of the wreck can provide some interesting invertebrate life that is easy to photograph.

Around the folded back doors and loose metal sheets you can locate a variety of organisms inactive during the day. Basket starfish cling to the roof of these

Typical Depth Range:
 30-60 ft (9-18 meters)
Typical Current Conditions: None
Typical Visibility: 50 ft (15 meters)
Expertise Required: Novice

artificial caverns. Typically, they appear as pale tan disks because their arms are folded around the central body. Coral shrimp, file clams and other residents seeking shelter can also be found in these protected alcoves.

Much sediment and rotting wood can be seen and exploration inside the wreck is not encouraged as bubbles not only reduce visibility by disturbing the accumulated mud, and also may cause the superstructure to collapse.

Nassau groupers found near the wreck are quite curious and may settle down with divers
to compare notes.

. The *Sayonara* rests among some very luxurious coral growth and away from the wreck you'll find plenty of marine life on the reef. Coral growth is typically distributed in discontinuous formations 10-20 ft across and about equally as high.

Most impressive here is the size and variability of emergent sponges. Giant basket and stinking vase sponges dwarf some of the coral formations. Basket sponges 4-5 ft high are common, together with yellow tube and bright red finger sponges. Red encrusting sponges are everywhere.

Modest fish populations may also be seen. There are always stoplight parrotfish, French, gray and queen angels. A host of barracudas frequent the area. Small schools of French grunts circulate among the reefs and occasionally peacock flounders rest camouflaged out on the sand flats.

37 Elbow

This popular dive site is found at Turneffe's southernmost promontory. Here the reef reverses its direction and is very exposed, deep and wide. Shallow reefs crest at 80 ft and deepen progressively toward the southern tip of the elbow-shaped promontory. Waters above the reefs have typically excellent visibility, with currents generally flowing from the north. However, their direction and strength are inconsistent and should be checked to plan your dive.

Typical Depth Range:
  60 ft (18 meters) to unlimited (wall)
Typical Current Conditions:
  Strong (2 knots)
Typical Visibility: 100 ft (30 meters)
Expertise Required: Advanced

F BUREK

Jacks patrol the water above the reef at the Elbow.

F.O. MEYER

Large schools of fish congregate at the Elbow, attracting exciting pelagics in mid-water.

The Elbow is considered an advanced dive because of environmental conditions. Seas are often rough even on calm days because of large ocean swells, making entries and exits more difficult. Once in the water, currents usually sweep divers out toward deep water, beyond the reef, and 75% of the dive time must be spent in mid-water because bottom time on the reefs at depth is very limited. Excellent buoyancy control and air consumption are simply a must. Depth, visibility, current and marine life conditions make this site better as a drift dive and more suited for wide-angle photography.

Like similar promontories elsewhere in the world, this site features abundant, large pelagics. Large congregations of snappers, horse-eye jacks and cubera snappers school feed in mid-water above the reefs. By looking in the canyons, divers can see large groupers lurking beneath a cover of soft corals and rocky coral ledges. Seasonal appearances of shark and kingfish add to the pelagic spectacle, but most spectacular is the majestic flight of eagle rays. On exceptional days a school of more than 50 eagle rays can bring a sensation of euphoria to even the most jaded and experienced diver.

38 Myrtle's Turtle

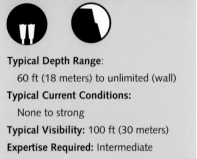

Typical Depth Range:
  60 ft (18 meters) to unlimited (wall)
Typical Current Conditions:
  None to strong
Typical Visibility: 100 ft (30 meters)
Expertise Required: Intermediate

Myrtle's Turtle is the first in a series of dive sites on the eastern limb of Turneffe Atoll. It is located just a short distance north of the Elbow and directly in line with the old lighthouse platform and two western points of Turneffe. It is among the best dive destinations Belize has to offer. Myrtle's Turtle is a deep dive and requires divers to monitor their depth and time carefully. The reef is fronted by a sheer wall that begins at 155 ft and plunges vertically to intersect a slope covered with sparse coral plates and sea whips at about 250 ft. Above the wall, the reef slopes upward steeply to form the seaward flank of a system of spurs and grooves that crest at 55 ft. Along the wall, living coral formations form huge triangular blocks and an uneven line of alternating ridges and narrow cuts up to 35 ft deep. These shelter a fantastic variety of tropical fish and invertebrates.

The growth of deep-water lace coral is especially impressive on coral ridges near the wall. Elegant stands of these deep red soft corals can lend both color and form to the foreground of wide-angle compositions. A little seaward and above the reef, schools of Spanish mackerels, horse-eye jacks, cubera snappers and permits commonly feed in mid-water. Also present may be small schools of eagle rays, creole mackerels and tuna.

A large green turtle, named Myrtle, has appeared consistantly in this part of the reef for the past 15 years. Myrtle is about 5-6 ft long and has grown accustomed to divers.

RICK TEGLER

Diver enjoys a deep dive at Myrtle's Turtle.

39 Black Beauty

Black Beauty is another site along the same eastern drop-off as Myrtle's Turtle. Once again, the reef top consists of a series of triangular slivers of living coral and deep sand-floored ravines, culminating in a straight line near the wall at about 60 ft. From there they dip steeply toward the wall and deep water.

The featured attraction at this site was a huge black coral "tree" found along the drop-off in shallow water. However, like many other large, shallow, black coral growths, this beautiful feature has succumbed to the unrelenting hunt and demand for black coral jewelry. Rarely are black coral trees now found here above 50 ft, leaving only scattered small trees growing along the steep reef slope above 150 ft.

Typical Depth Range:
 60 ft (18 meters) to unlimited (wall)
Typical Current Conditions:
 None to strong
Typical Visibility: 80 ft (24 meters)
Expertise Required: Intermediate

Although black coral growths are few, this site still has much to offer. Large pelagics frequent the wall and more than 40 kinds of other fish live among the rugged coral terrain. The ridges consist of beautiful coral growth and shelter many species of marine life.

Princess parrotfish use their strong beaks to help keep algae from overwhelming the coral.

Rope sponges and soft corals along vertical walls create interesting forms for photographs.

40 Lefty's Ledge

The straight eastern reef line south of Black Beauty forms a small scallop at Lefty's Ledge. All along the rim are massive coral bastions and at several locations seaward, coral growths create prominent ledges that jut out above the deep-water drop-off. Behind the curved rim, the reef is deeply incised with sandy canyons that slope seaward and spill out over the drop-offs at 100 ft. Most sandy strips are relatively narrow features littered with small coral structures, but one looks like a jet runway because of its enormous width and length. This combination of craggy reefs and open sand flats creates a range of environments suitable for many different kinds of marine life.

Pelagics are often attracted to an area because of an abundance of food or suit-

Typical Depth Range:
  50 ft (15 meters) to unlimited (wall)
Typical Current Conditions: None to strong
Typical Visibility: 80 ft (24 meters)
Expertise Required: Intermediate

able shelter. Lefty's Ledge provides both, so pelagics are the main attraction. Perhaps as many as 50 kinds of fish can be seen here on a single dive by exploring the reef and keeping an eye on the open sea. All along the sloping drop-off, you can encounter schools of horse-eye jacks, bar

The black spot on the four-eye butterflyfish's tail confuses potential predators.

jacks, Spanish mackerels, creole wrasses, yellowtail snappers and permits. Eagle rays, ocean triggerfish and barracudas can also be seen, along with occasional appearances of hammerhead, black tip and bull sharks.

Photographers will find it easy to shoot several rolls above and along the reef, featuring blue chromis, striped grunts, mutton snappers, black durgons, blue tangs, damselfish, groupers and parrotfish.

Plenty of other marine life can draw attention from the parade of fish. Near the wall and on the ledges are gorgeous growths of deep-water lace coral and interesting formations of boulder or sheet coral. On all parts of the reef, boring, emergent and encrusting sponges create decorative forms and add rich warm colors to photographs. As you move in and out of coral formations and across the reef top, you may find large hermit crabs, Pederson Cleaner shrimp stations, browsing flamingo tongues and orange crinoids. Wherever you dive at Lefty's Ledge, you will always be richly rewarded.

41 Majestic Point

Majestic Point is a small promontory formed by a massive coral ridge. Its coral buttresses rise vertically about 55 ft from the steep drop-off found all along the eastern reefs on Turneffe's southern end. On either side of this majestic spur are other well-developed coral ridges separated by sandy crevices. The sand channels generally run perpendicular to the reef line, but some turn and intersect the reef at acute angles near the drop-off.

Typical Depth Range:
   50 ft (15 meters) to unlimited (wall)
Typical Current Conditions:
   None to moderate
Typical Visibility: 80 ft (24 meters)
Expertise Required: Intermediate

Like similar areas to the south near Myrtle's Turtle, there are plenty of deep-water lace coral and gaudy sponges on the massive coral ridge. Many lace corals form huge fans more than 6 ft across. These sessile carnivores and filter-feeding basket, giant tube and rope sponges thrive because they have good exposure to plankton that is swept along the reef front by currents.

The promontory is very photogenic and can be the focus of most of your dive. Late morning sun bathes the decorative cover,

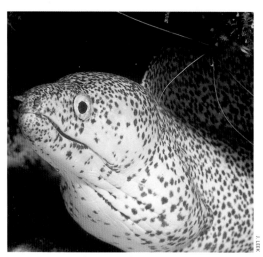

Spotted moray eel at Majestic Point.

divers or large pelagics in golden rays and the point is surrounded by streams of light when you look upward toward the early afternoon sun. This allows you to capture the effect of sunbeams being filtered by lace coral, or frame a diver dwarwfed by the impressive presence of the point.

42 Front Porch

Directly east off the front porch of Turneffe Island Lodge is another site along the same eastern reef line, northward of Majestic Point. Like its neighbor, this site has a deep and high relief reef. Its top at 55 ft is about the same depth as Majestic Point, but here fewer canyons extend through the reef all the way to the drop-off and none of the coral ridges are exaggerated in size.

Coral growth is vigorous and fresh here and, as everywhere else along this part of the reef trend, it forms many protective recesses that shelter a host of large and small creatures. Fish are quite prolific at Front Porch and several curious forms may be discovered within the darkened nooks.

Typical Depth Range:
  50 ft (15 meters) to unlimited (wall)
Typical Current Conditions:
  None to moderate
Typical Visibility: 80 ft (24 meters)
Expertise Required: Intermediate

One resident found here, which is not particularly common elsewhere in the Caribbean, is the dark blue toadfish. Its body is completely covered with white or

A nocturnal predator, the red hind is usually found resting in the reefs by day.

B. OPPEN

With graceful lines and brilliant red color, rope sponges add interest to diver portraits along the wall at Front Porch.

light blue spots except around the eyes where a series of short lines highlight a star pattern. Some divemasters in the area erroneously identify this fish as a stargazer, but its bearded large mouth, body shape and its sound distinguish it as a species of toadfish. Many divers who have not seen this fish have heard its distinctive croaking noise, similar to, yet different from the grunting noise made by grouper. Although a shy fish, some divemasters have managed to coax it out of its hiding place to give photographers a most rewarding memento of the reef.

43 Gailes Point

Gailes Point is one of those dive sites along the eastern reef line that has everything. The reef line sweeps inward toward the lagoon and forms a shallow crescent several hundred yards across and perhaps 50 yards deep. On either side of the reentrant is a massive coral ridge that forms a distinctive point. The reef top slopes gently seaward at 45 ft. It consists of poorly defined spurs and grooves that coalesce and become increasingly rugged near the drop-off.

Overhangs and caverns can be found all along and near the drop-off, including several large caverns at 70 ft on the northern coral ridge, which flanks the recessed reef line. These shelter large groupers and nurse sharks. This part of the reef may well be a grouper mating

Typical Depth Range:
45 ft (14 meters) to unlimited (wall)
Typical Current Conditions:
None to moderate
Typical Visibility: 80 ft (24 meters)
Expertise Required: Intermediate

site, as a large number of Nassau, black, tiger and marble groupers can be seen here in early December.

The broad sand flats behind the reefs (along the drop-off) are popular feeding areas for spotted eagle rays looking for crustaceans. The drop-off is a superb place for working with a model to shoot exciting "diver-with-spotted-eagle-ray" shots.

Although the presence of large pelagics can be totally consuming, this site has much more to offer. The stony coral is especially well developed here and some of the narrow dark crevices are crowded with sponge and soft coral. Clusters of bryozoans, encrusting sponges and tunicates are other great photo subjects found under ledges and on the shadowed walls of crevices. On the reef top, filefish, butterflyfish and trumpetfish find the abundant reef recesses comforting.

Deep parts of the reef offer still more variety. Thickets of deep-water lace coral, scattered growths of black coral and scroll coral grace the sloping drop-off below 60 ft.

From bottom to top, this reef has enough attractions to satisfy even the most discriminating diver. One dive is simply not sufficient to capture all that is here.

J. BUREK

Yellow pencil corals grow in shallow reefs.

Hazardous Marine Life

F.O. MEYER

Fire Coral Mustard brown in color, fire coral is most often found in shallower waters encrusting and taking the shape of dead gorgonians or coral. It forms multiple branches that are usually smooth and cylindrical and dotted with little holes, out of which the hair-like polyps protrude. Upon contact, the nematocysts (small stinging cells located on the polyps) discharge, causing a burning sensation that lasts for several minutes and can sometime cause red welts on the skin. If you brush against fire coral, do not try to rub the affected area as you will spread the small stinging particles. Cortisone cream can reduce inflammation and minor abrasions can be treated with meat tenderizer and antibiotic cream. Serious cuts should be treated by a doctor.

Fire coral

110

Sponges They may be beautiful, but sponges can also pack a powerful punch with fine spicules that sting on contact. Differentiating between sponges can be a difficult task, but just remember that the bright red sponges often carry the most potent sting, although they are not the only culprits. If you touch a stinging sponge, scrape the area with the edge of a sharp knife. Home remedies include mild vinegar or ammonia solutions to ease the pain. Regardless, the pain usually goes away within a day and again, cortisone cream can help.

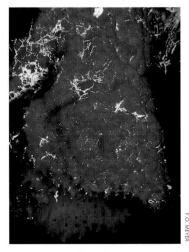
Sponge

Sea Urchins Long-spined sea urchins are abundant in the Caribbean and are recognizable by their black bodies and long needle-like spines. The urchin's dangerous weapon is its spines, which can penetrate neoprene wetsuits, booties and gloves with ease. You'll know you've been jabbed by the instant pain.

Long-spined sea urchin

Urchins tend to be more common in shallow areas near shore and come out of their shelters under coral heads at night. Minor punctures can be treated by extracting the spines and treating the wound with antibiotic cream. More serious injuries should be treated by a doctor.

Bristle Worms Also called fire worms, bristle worms can be found on most reefs with little searching. Bristle worms have segmented bodies that are covered with either tufts or bundles of sensory hairs that extend in tiny, sharp, detachable bristles. If

Green bristle worm

you touch one with bare skin the tiny, stinging bristles embed in your skin and cause a burning sensation that may be followed by a red spot or welt. The bristles will eventually work their way out of your skin in a couple of days or you can try to scrape them off with the edge of a knife.

Sea Wasps A potentially serious diving hazard also known as box jellies, sea wasps are small, potent jellyfish with four stinging tentacles. Distinguished by their rectangular-shaped dome, with their long tentacles dangling from each of the four corners, sea wasps generally swim within a few feet from the surface at night. If they have been spotted

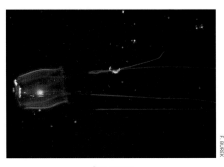

Sea wasp

in the water where you are planning a night dive, take caution. Do not linger on the surface upon entry and when resurfacing, turn off your dive light as it attracts them and get out of the water quickly. The sting is very painful and leaves a red welt. If you are allergic to bee stings, consider foregoing the dive, as you will most likely have the same reaction to a sea wasp sting.

Scorpionfish They may be one of the sea's best camouflaged creatures, but if you are punctured by the poisonous spine hidden among its fins, you'll know you've found a scorpionfish. Most commonly found in Belize, the spotted scorpionfish is distinguished by the bright white spots found on the backside of its pectoral fins.

Scorpionfish

Unlike other scorpionfish, it doesn't necessarily possess the large appendages (*cirri*) or "plumes" above its eyes. Scorpionfish tend to lie on the bottom or on coral, so as long as you practice good buoyancy control and watch where you put your hands, you shouldn't have a problem. Should you get stung, go to a hospital or a doctor as soon as possible because the sting can result in severe allergic reactions; pain and infection are almost guaranteed.

Stingrays Recognized by their diamond-shaped body, and wide "wings," the stingray has one or two venomous spines at the base of its long tail. Most commonly found in Belize waters are the southern stingray, which has a pointed snout and pointed wingtips, and the yellow stingray, whose snout and wings are rounded. Generally staying put on the sandy floor around reefs, these creatures are harmless unless you sit or step on them. If you harass them, you may discover the long, barbed stinger at the base of the tail. Wounds are always extremely painful, often deep and infective, and can cause serious symptoms like anaphylactic shock. If you get stung, head for a hospital immediately. The best policy with stingrays is to leave them alone and they'll leave you alone.

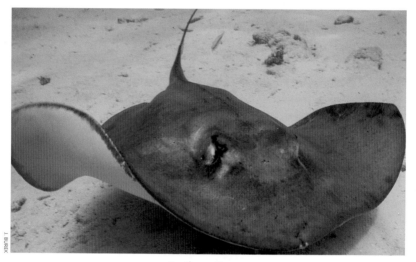

Southern stingray

Eels Recognizable by their long, thick, snake-like body and tapered head, eels abide by the agreement not to bother you, unless you bother them. It is best not to feed them, especially when you don't know if other eels or hazardous fish are in the area. Eels have extremely poor eyesight and cannot always distinguish between food and your hand.

Chain moray

Likewise, don't put your hand in a dark hole, because it just might house an angry eel. If you are bitten, don't try to pull your hand away as their teeth are extraordinarily sharp. Let the eel release it and then surface slowly, apply first aid and head for the nearest hospital.

Sharks Sharks come in a variety of shapes and sizes, many of which are seen in Belizean waters. Sharks, like rays, are considered cartilaginous fish, which means their skeletons are composed of cartilage as opposed to bone. They are most recognizable by their triangular dorsal fin. Perhaps more than any other fish species, sharks demand that

Nurse shark

divers practice common sense and respect. Sharks will generally not attack unless provoked, so don't taunt, tease or feed them. Encountering a shark is a thrilling treat for any diver and can be an exciting, mutually respectful experience. But be careful, because you never know when a shark might be grumpy. Any shark injury obviously calls for immediate medical attention.

Barracuda Barracudas are identifiable by their long, silver, cylindrical body and razor-like teeth protruding out of an underslung jaw. They swim alone or in small groups, continually opening and closing their mouths to assist respiration. Reports of the barracuda's ferocity are often unfounded as, although unnervingly curious,

Barracuda

they are actually somewhat shy. They will hover near divers to observe them, but try to photograph barracudas and they keep their distance. The only substantiated barracuda incidents involve spearfishing so again, don't bother them, and they won't bother you.

Diving Conservation & Awareness

F. BUREK

Reef Etiquette

Dive sites tend to be located where the reefs and walls display the most beautiful corals and sponges. It only takes a moment—an inadvertently placed hand or knee on the coral or an unaware brush or kick with a fin—to destroy this fragile living part of our delicate ecosystem. Please consider the following tips when diving and help preserve the ecology and beauty of the reefs:

1. Maintain proper buoyancy control and avoid over-weighting. Be aware that buoyancy can change over the period of an extended trip: initially you may breathe harder and need more weighting; a few days later you may breath more easily and need less weight.

2. Use correct weight belt position to stay horizontal, i.e., raise the belt above your waist to elevate your feet/fins, and move the belt lower toward your hips to lower feet/fins.

3. Use your tank position in the backpack as a balance weight, i.e., raise your backpack on the tank to lower your legs, and lower the backpack on the tank to raise your legs.

4. Be careful about buoyancy loss at depth; the deeper you go the more your wetsuit compresses, and the more buoyancy you lose.

5. Photographers must be extra careful. Cameras and equipment affect buoyancy. Changing f-stops, framing a subject, and maintaining position for a photo often conspire to prohibit the ideal "no-touch" approach on a reef. So, when you must use "holdfasts," choose them intelligently, i.e. use one finger only for leverage off an area of dead coral.

Turtle Conservation

Throughout the world there are eight species of sea turtles, three of which inhabit the coast of Belize. All are endangered.

The green turtle (*Chelonia mydas*), named for the greenish color of its fat, can grow to more than 4 ft in length and attain a weight well over 600 pounds. These turtles have been decimated by hunters (used as the main ingredient in turtle soup) and by the destruction of seagrass, their main food source.

The loggerhead (*Caretta caretta*) has a large head, short neck and a heart-shaped, reddish-brown shell. Due to a precarious reproduction cycle, animal predators, human intervention and poachers, only about 5% of the turtle's eggs actually survive.

The hawksbill (*Eretmochelys imbricata*) has a narrow bill and a sharp pointed beak. Its shell is not solid, but made up of bony overlapping orange, brown and gold scales. The beautiful shell, however, is the reason for its endangerment: sea hunters capture hawksbills to be stuffed and displayed as trophies, or to strip their scales into tortoise shell combs, jewelry and eyeglass frames.

What can you do to help turtles survive?

√ Don't disturb or frighten a sea turtle, especially during mating season (June through August).

√ Don't eat turtle eggs, turtle soup or any other turtle dish.

√ Don't buy or use any product made from turtle shell.

√ Encourage efforts to preserve turtle-nesting beaches as natural reserves.

KEVIN SCHAFER

Hawksbill turtle

6. Avoid full leg kicks when working close to the bottom and when leaving a photo scene. When you inadvertently kick something, stop kicking! This seems obvious, but some divers either semi-panic or are totally oblivious when they bump something. When treading water in shallow reef areas, take care not to kick up clouds of sand. Settling sand can easily smother the delicate organisms of the reef.

7. When swimming in strong currents, be extra careful about leg kicks and handholds.

8. Attach dangling gauges, computer consoles and octopus regulators. They are like miniature wrecking balls to a reef.

9. Never drop boat anchors onto a coral reef and take care not to ground boats on coral. Encourage dive operators and regulatory bodies to establish permanent moorings at popular dive sites.

10. Resist the temptation to collect or buy corals or shells. Aside from the ecological damage, taking home marine souvenirs depletes the beauty of a site and spoils the enjoyment of others.

11. Resist the temptation to feed fish. You may disturb their normal eating habits, encourage aggressive behavior, or feed them food that is detrimental to their health.

Marine Conservation Organizations

Coral reefs and oceans are facing unprecedented environmental pressures. The following groups are actively involved in promoting responsible diving practices, publicizing environmental marine threats and lobbying for better policies.

Project AWARE Foundation
☎ 714-540-0251
website: www.projectaware.org

CORAL: The Coral Reef Alliance
☎ 510-848-0110
website: www.coral.org/

Coral Forest
☎ 415-788-REEF
website: www.blacktop.com/coral-forest/

Cousteau Society
☎ 757-523-9335
website: www.cousteau.org

Ocean Futures
☎ 714-456-0790
website: www.oceanfutures.org

ReefKeeper International
☎ 305-358-4600
website: www.reefkeeper.org

Listings

F.O. MEYER

Tourist Information

Belize Tourist Board
83 N. Front St.
PO Box 325
Belize City
☎ (2) 77213, 73255
fax (2) 77490

Belize Tourism Industry Association
10 N. Park
PO Box 62
Belize City
☎ (2) 75717, 78709

Belize On-Line

For a small country with a primitive telephone system, Belize has embraced the Internet with surprising speed and success. Many Belizean businesses are reachable by electronic mail (often in the format *businessname*@btl.net) and there are several useful websites including:

www.ambergriscaye.com
Great information about San Pedro and diving on Ambergris.

www.belize.com
Belize online tourism and investment guide.

www.belizebusiness.com
Features a directory of Belize businesses.

www.belizeit.com
Belize Tourism Industry Association web site.

www.belizenet.com
Good topside and trip planning information.

Dive Services

The following dive services are available on Ambergris Caye. Look under the Accommodations listings for dive services on the atoll resorts. Whether you stay on the mainland or offshore, you will discover that most hotels, travel agencies and dive shops can easily arrange snorkeling or scuba diving trips.

To call Belize, dial the international access code for the country you are calling from (in the U.S. it's 011), +501 before dialing the 6-digit local number.

Adventures in Watersports
☎ 26-3844
fax: 26-3707
email: advwtrspts@btl.net

Amigos Del Mar Dive Shop
☎ 26-2706/800-346-6116
fax: 26-2648
email: amigosdive@btl.net

Belize Dive Center
☎ 26-2797/800-938-0860
email: bzedivectr@btl.net

Blue Hole Dive Center
☎ 26-2982
email: bluehole@btl.net

Coral Beach Dive Club
☎ 26-2013
fax: 26-2864
email: forman@btl.net

Discovery Divers
☎ 26-3484
fax: 26-2881
email: discovery@btl.net

Fantasea Scuba School & Watersports
☎ 26-2576
fax: 26-2576
email: fantasea@btl.net

Hustler Tours
☎ 26-2538/2279
fax: 26-2719

Gaz Cooper's Dive Belize
☎ 26-3202/800-499-3002
fax: 954-351-9740
email: gaz@btl.net

Paradise Dive Shop
☎ 26-2797
fax: 26-2797
email: paradive@btl.net

Ramon's Dive Shop
☎ 26-2071/800-624-4215
fax: 601-649-1996
email: ramons@c-gate.net

Reef Divers Belize Ltd.
☎ 26-3134
fax: 26-2943
email: reefdivers@btl.net

Live-Aboards

The following live-aboards all feature 7-day trips that include 5 days of diving.

Aggressor Fleet Ltd.
The Belize Aggressor III
boat length: 120 ft
passengers: 18
☎ 800-348-2628
fax: 504-384-0817
email: divboat@aol.com
website: www.aggressor.com

Peter Hughes
Peter Hughes Wave Dancer
boat length: 120 ft
passengers: 20
☎ 800-932-6237
fax: 305-669-9475
email: dancer@peterhughes.com
website: www.peterhughes.com

Oceanwide Expeditions
Rembrandt van Rijn
boat length: 184 ft
passengers: 32
☎ 800-453-7245
fax: 713-591-1082
website: www.diveguideint.com/p0875.htm
email: oceanwh@infohwy.com

Accommodations

Ambergris Caye

Barrier Reef Hotel
☎ 26-2075
fax: 26-2719
email: barriereef@btl.net

Caribe Island Resort
☎ 26-3233
fax: 26-3399
email: ccaribe@btl.net

Caribbean Villas
☎ 26-2715
fax: 26-2885
email: c-v-hotel@btl.net

Casa Solana
☎ 26-2100
fax: 26-2855
email: casasolana@btl.net

Coconuts Caribbean Hotel
☎ 26-3500
fax: 26-3501
email: coconuts@btl.net

Conch Shell Hotel
☎ 26-2062
fax: 26-3849
email: conchshell@snet.net

Coral Beach Hotel & Dive Club
☎ 26-2013
fax: 26-2864
email: forman@btl.net

Corona Del Mar
☎ 26-2055
fax: 26-2461
email: corona@btl.net

Hideaway Sports Lodge
☎ 26-2141
fax: 26-2269
email: hideaway@btl.net

Journey's End
☎ 26-2054/800-460-5665
fax: 26-2397
email: journeysend@journeysendresort.com

Mata Rocks Resort
☎ 26-2336/888-628-2757
fax: 26-2349
email: matarocks@btl.net

Mayan Princess
☎ 26-2778
fax: 26-2784
email: mayanprin@btl.net

Paradise Hotel
☎ 26-2083
fax: 26-2797
email: paradive@btl.net

Ramon's Village
☎ 26-2071/800-624-4215
fax: 601-649-1996
email: ramons@c-gate.net

Rocks Inn
☎ 26-2326
fax: 26-2358
email: rocks@btl.net

Royal Palm Villas
☎ 26-2244
fax: 26-2063
email: royalplam@btl.net

Rubies Hotel
☎ 26-2063
fax: 26-2063
email: rubys@btl.net

San Pedro Holiday Hotel
☎ 26-2014
fax: 26-2295
email: holiday@btl.net

Sand's Hotel
☎ 26-2510
fax: 26-2618

SunBreeze Beach Hotel
☎ 26-2191
fax: 26-2251
email: sunbreeze@btl.net

The Villas at Banyan Bay
☎ 26-3739
fax: 26-2766

Victoria House Resort
☎ 26-2067
fax: 26-2429
email: victoria@btl.net

Turneffe Atoll

Turneffe Island Lodge
☎ 21-2011/800-874-0118
fax: 770-534-8290
email: info@turneffelodge.com
website: www.turneffelodge.com

Turneffe Flats
☎ 21-2046/800-815-1304
fax: 605-578-7540
email: flats@blackhills.com
website: www.tflats.com

Blackbird Caye Resort
☎ 23-2767/888-271-3483
fax: 310-937-6473
email: dive@blackbirdresort.com
website: blackbirdresort.com

Glover's Reef

Manta Resort
☎ 23-1895/800-326-1724
fax: 310-937-6473
email: info@ mantaresort.com
website: www.mataresort.com

Lighthouse Reef

Lighthouse Reef Resort
☎ 23-1205/800-423-3114
fax: 941-439-2118
email: reservations@scubabelize.com

Common Marine Life of Belize

INVERTEBRATE ANIMALS
Sponges (Porifera)

basket sponge: *Xestospongia muta*
giant yellow tube sponge: *Verongia fistularis*
iridescent tube sponge: *Spinosella plicifera*
red boring sponge: *Clinoa delitrix*
lavender vase sponge: *Callyspongia plicifera*
vase sponge: *Dasychalina cyathina*
stinking vase sponge: *Ircina campana*
red finger sponge: *Haliclona rubens*

Corals and Anemones (Cnidaria)

Anemones

giant Caribbean anemone: *Condylactis gigantea*
giant green anemone: *Anthopleura xanthogrammica*
ringed anemone: *Bartholomea annulata*

True Corals

Soft Corals (Gorgonacea)
  sea fans: *Gorgonia spp., Iciligorgia schrammi* (deep-water sea fan)
  sea feathers and sea plumes: *Pseudopterogorgia spp.*
  sea rods: *Plexaura spp., Eunicea spp.* (knobby candelabrum), *Briarum abestinum* (corky sea fingers)
  sea whips: *Pterogorgia spp.*
Hard Corals (Sceractinia)
  Boulder-shaped corals:
    boulder coral: *Montastrea annularis*
    large-cupped boulder coral: *Montastrea cavernosa*
    depressed brain coral: *Diploria labyrinthiformis*
    sharp-hilled brain coral: *D. clivosa*
    common brain coral: *D. strigosa*
    giant brain coral: *Colpophyllis natans*
    mustard hill coral: *Porites astreoides*
    meandrine brain coral: *Meandrina meandrites*
  Branching Corals:
    elkhorn coral: *Acropora palmata*
    staghorn coral: *A. cervicornis*
    pillar coral: *Dendrogyra cylindrus*
    yellow pencil coral: *Madracis mirabilis*
  Others: Encrusting, Plate-like and Flower Corals:
    flower coral: *Eusmilia fastigiata*

grooved fungus coral: *Mycetophyllia ferox*
large cactus coral: *M. lamarckiana*
scroll coral: *Agaricia undata*
tan lettuce-leaf coral: *A. agaricites*
polygonal coral: *Isophyllastrea rigida*
wire coral: *Stichopathes lutkeni*

Hydrocorals (Milliporina)
fire corals: *Millepora spp.*

Black Coral (Antipatharia)
black coral: *Antipathes spp.*

Mollusks

rough file clam: *Lima scabra*
reef octopus: *Octopus briareus*
flamingo tongue: *Cyphoma gibbosum*

Crustaceans

arrow crab: *Stenorhynchus seticornis*
star-eyed hermit crab: *Dardanus venosus*
Pederson's Cleaner shrimp: *Periclimenes pedersoni*
banded coral shrimp: *Stenopus hispidus*
spotted brown shrimp: *Thor ambionesis*
spanish lobster: *Scyllarides aequinoctialis*
spiny lobster: *Panulirus argus*

Echinoderms

basketstar: *Astrophyton muricatum*
Suenson's brittle star: *Ophiothrix suensonii*
Oersted's brittle star: *O. oestedii*
ruby brittle star: *Ophioderma rubicundum*
long-spined sea urchin: *Diadema antillarum*
reef urchin: *Echinometra viridis*
lion's paw sea cucumber: *Holothuria thomasi*
swimming crinoid: *Analcidometra cribbea*
orange sea lily: *Nemaster rubiginosa*

VERTEBRATE ANIMALS
Fishes

Sharks and Rays

manta ray: *Manta birostris*
eagle ray: *Aetobatus narinari*
spotted eagle ray: *Actobatus narinari*
hammerhead sharks: *Sphyrna spp.*
tiger shark: *Guleocerdo cuvieri*
blacktip shark: *Carcharhinus brevipinna*
lemon shark: *Negaprion brevirostris*
nurse shark: *Ginglymostoma cirratum*

Bony Fishes

foureye butterflyfish: *Chaetodon capistratus*
banded butterflyfish: *C. striatus*
french angelfish: *Pomacanthus paru*
gray angelfish: *P. arcuatus*
rock beauty: *Holacanthus tricolor*
queen angelfish: *H. ciliaris*
horse-eye jack: *Caranx latus*
bar jack: *C. ruber*
permit: *Trachinotus falcutus*

tiger grouper: *Mycteroperca tigris*
black grouper: *M. bonaci*
marbled grouper: *Epinephelus inermis*
Nassau grouper: *E. striatus*
coney: *E. fulvus*
graysby: *E. cruentatus*
rock hind: *E. adscensionis*
red hind: *E. guttatus*

fairy basslet: *Gramma loreto*
blackcap basslet: *G. melacra*
indigo hamlet: *Hypoplectrus indigo*

bluestriped grunt: *Haemulon sciurus*
french grunt: *H. flavolineatum*
grey snapper: *Lutjanus analis*
cubera snapper: *L. cyanopterus*
yellowtail snapper: *Ocyurus chysurus*

black durgon: *Melichthys niger*
ocean triggerfish: *Canthidermis sufflamen*

queen triggerfish: *Balistes vetula*
scrawled filefish: *Aluterus scriptus*
whitespotted filefish: *Cantherhines macroceros*
honeycomb cowfish: *Lactophrys polygonia*
smooth trunkfish: *L. triqueter*

neon goby: Gobiosoma oceanops
sharknose goby: *G. evelynae*

threespot damselfish: *Eupomacentrus planifrons*
dusky damselfish: *E. dorsopunicans*
sergeant major: *Abudefduf saxatilis*
blue cromis: *Chromis cyanea*

stoplight parrotfish: *Sparisoma viride*
redband parrotfish: *S. aurofrenatum*
queen parrotfish: *Scarus vetula*
blue parrotfish: *S. coeruleus*
rainbow parrotfish: *S. quacamaia*
striped parrotfish: *S. croicencis*

spotted moray eel: *Gymnothorax moringa*
green moray eel: *G. flavimarginatus*
garden eel: *Nystactichths halis*

spotted drum: *Equetus punctatus*
jackknife fish: *E. lanceolatus*

barracuda: *Sphyraena barracuda*
yellowhead jawfish: *Opistognathus aurifrons*
yellow chub: *Kyphosus incisor*
tarpon: *Megalops atlanticus*
creole wrasse: *Clepticus parrai*
blue tang: *Acanthurus coeruleus*
sand diver: *Synodus intermedius*
tilefish: *Malacanthus plumieri*
trumpetfish: *Aulostomus maculatus*
peacock flounder: *Bothus lunatus*
squirrelfish: *Holocentrus rufus*

Index

dive sites covered in this book appear in **bold** type